Routledge Revivals

Politics and Progress

In *Politics and Progress*, Muir aims to outline the political and social aims of liberalism and how it differs from conservatism and socialism as well as philosophising what a truly liberal society would look like. Originally published in 1923, this study details the political situation as it stood then, the past achievements of liberalism and what immediate problems society is facing that need to solved. This title will be of interest to students of politics.

Politics and Progress

A Survey of the Problems of Today

Ramsay Muir

Routledge
Taylor & Francis Group

First published in 1923
by Methuen & Co. Ltd

This edition first published in 2016 by Routledge
2 Park Square, Milton Park, Abingdon, Oxon, OX14 4RN
and by Routledge
711 Third Avenue, New York, NY 10017

Routledge is an imprint of the Taylor & Francis Group, an informa business

Publisher's Note
The publisher has gone to great lengths to ensure the quality of this reprint but points out that some imperfections in the original copies may be apparent.

Disclaimer
The publisher has made every effort to trace copyright holders and welcomes correspondence from those they have been unable to contact.

A Library of Congress record exists under LC control number: 23011402

ISBN 13: 978-1-138-64156-3 (hbk)
ISBN 13: 978-1-315-63040-3 (ebk)
ISBN 13: 978-1-138-64158-7 (pbk)

POLITICS AND PROGRESS

A SURVEY OF THE PROBLEMS OF TO-DAY

BY

RAMSAY MUIR

METHUEN & CO. LTD.
36 ESSEX STREET W.C.
LONDON

First Published in 1923

PRINTED IN GREAT BRITAIN

TO

MY FRIENDS IN ROCHDALE

PREFACE

THE purpose of this little book is to give a coherent view of the political and social aims of Liberalism; to show that it represents a distinctive attitude, sharply contrasted with that of Conservatism and with that of Socialism; to analyse the reasons for the Liberal's dissatisfaction with the existing order of things; to describe the kind of society which he would desire to create, and the immediate steps towards this goal which he would advocate; and to show that these aims are in accord with the traditions and the great achievements of British Liberalism.

More than two years ago, after profitable discussions with a group of Manchester friends, I wrote a little book called "Liberalism and Industry." In a modest way I believe that it helped to stimulate an active discussion among the younger Liberals, which has gone forward without interruption during these two years. From this discussion I have learnt much; and in the present volume some of the conclusions which I tentatively put forward in the earlier book have been considerably modified. But this book is not meant in any sense as a new edition of "Liberalism and Industry." Most of the subjects dealt with in that book, and especially in its first half, are here dealt with very lightly, or not at all; and the ground covered by this volume is much wider than the ground covered by its predecessor.

Nor is this little book to be regarded in any sense

as a pronouncement on behalf of a group or clique within the Liberal party. I am proud to be associated with a body of men who have been giving much of their time and thought to the co-operative discussion of some of the most difficult of political problems. But their aim has throughout been primarily investigative and educative. They repudiate the suggestion that they form a clique or school within the Liberal party. And, in any case, what I have here written, though it has been deeply influenced by what I have learnt in these discussions, is issued solely on my own responsibility.

RAMSAY MUIR

CONTENTS

POLITICS AND PROGRESS

CHAPTER I

THE ALIGNMENT OF PARTIES

I. THE POLITICAL SITUATION IN 1923

THE General Election of 1922 will probably be regarded, by future historians, as marking the definite beginning of a new era in British politics. Throughout the century of strenuous political activity which preceded the Great War, both Parliament and the country were broadly divided between two great political forces—a party of Conservation and a party of Progress. In the party of Progress there were always—as was natural—various and even conflicting elements. But on the whole they held together, and combined to maintain successive ministries in power. Even when a distinct Labour party was organized in 1900, it was content for a number of years to act as a wing of the Liberal party, which could count upon its steady support during the sharp conflicts of 1910–1914. The division of the political forces of the country into two main armies was so well established that it seemed to be almost part of the order of Nature. Our whole machinery of government took it for granted, and seemed to be workable only on the assumption that this division continued. The very arrangement of the seats in the House of Commons implied it.

But the Great War, which has changed so many things, brought to an end this traditional alignment of political forces. During the war community of purpose almost obliterated party distinctions. After the war a large section of the Liberal party joined with the Conservatives to continue the device of Coalition Government, which had been adopted for war purposes; and used all the prestige of victory, and all the devices of electioneering, to destroy that section of the Liberal party which strove to maintain its independent existence Ruling for four years with an overwhelming majority in Parliament, the Coalition drove into the minds of a great part of the electorate, and especially into the minds of the younger voters whose political memory did not extend beyond the war, a belief that there was no fundamental difference between Liberalism and Conservatism. The small remnant of Liberals who stood aloof from the Coalition did little to weaken this belief. Their numbers in Parliament were insignificant, and wholly disproportionate to the support which they could count upon in the country. They were bereft of most of their leaders, and had few spokesmen who could command the ear of the country. They devoted themselves rather to criticism of the Government than to the promulgation of an inspiring policy of constructive reform; and even the criticism of so small a body was not very effective. It seemed that the once powerful Liberal party had sunk to impotence, and was on the verge of annihilation.

The young Labour party, which, having never faced the difficult task of government, was not handicapped by any record of imperfect achievement, naturally drew immense advantage from these circumstances. It had obtained control, for political purposes, of the powerful organization of trade unions and co-operative societies. It drew into its ranks multitudes of the younger and more progressive Liberals, who had lost patience with the policy of mere negation and criticism to which the shattered Liberal party seemed to be committed. It could appeal to all that vague yearning for a new heaven and a new earth, which inspired many men after the horrors of the war. It had a vision of a wholly new order—a vague and ill-thought-out vision, but still a vision ; and it could promulgate large promises all the more easily because its leaders had little experience of the difficulties of practical politics, and because there was no immediate prospect of their being called upon to translate their promises into facts.

It was in these circumstances that the election of 1922 took place. After four years peace had not been attained and Europe was threatened with bankruptcy. Trade was very bad, and unemployment more rife than it had been in living memory. The promises of a happier era, which had been given and accepted at the end of the war, had been bitterly disappointed. There was even a threat of a new war. The Coalition was discredited, and the Conservatives, who had been its main support, seized the opportunity to throw over the Liberals with whom they had acted, leaving them to bear the responsibility for all that had gone wrong, and came forward as the apostles of tranquillity. This skilful electioneering move left both wings of the Liberal party in a sad quandary. The Coalition Liberals were in a helpless predicament—deserted by their recent allies, and on bad terms with their former friends. The Independent Liberals were in an equally unhappy plight. Having given all their energy to fulminating against the Coalition, they found themselves deprived of their expected target; and they had no clearly defined constructive programme to advocate. The Labour party, on the other hand, welcomed and used a heaven-sent opportunity. They could contend that both of the traditional parties had failed, and that there was nothing to choose between them; they declared war against both alike, but more especially against the Liberals, hoping to achieve the final destruction of that historic party, and to take its place as the sole alternative to the Conservative party. As for the Liberals, cleft by bitter dissensions, deprived of their plans of campaign, and lacking any clear grounds on which to appeal to the electors, they were exposed to attack on both sides. It would not have been surprising if they had been wiped out, especially as the electoral system told against them with peculiar severity. They lost heavily to both of their opponents; for many advanced Liberals voted for Labour candidates in despair, and many voted Conservative lest the Labour party should triumph.

Yet even in these circumstances the result showed that the country was not unevenly divided between the three political parties. In so confused a battle as this election, totals of votes are apt to be misleading. But, for what they were worth, they showed that the Conservatives had obtained about five and a half millions of votes, against four and a quarter millions cast for the Labour party, and over four millions cast for the divided sections of the Liberal party. In other words, the two-party system had definitely disappeared. Henceforth we have to do with three parties, if not with four; and it has become a primary duty of every citizen to determine in which of these competing arrays he is to enrol himself.

For this reason it has become a matter of the first moment that not merely the immediate programmes, but the permanent attitudes and outlooks of these three parties should be clearly defined. The need is greatest in the case of the Liberal party, both because of the confusion into which it has been thrown by the events we have summarized, and also because it is no longer sufficient to describe Liberalism as "the party of progress," since that title is equally claimed by the Labour party. It has become essential to define the principles and aims of Liberalism in such a way as to make it plain either that Liberalism represents a quite distinctive attitude, differing equally from that of Conservatism and from that of the Labour party, or that it is merely a sort of compromise or half-way house, a "middle party" of "moderate men" with no characteristic or definable standpoint of its own.

II. THE TRIANGLE OF PARTIES

If we are driven to the second conclusion, then it is safe to say that there is no future for Liberalism. A "middle party"—even several "middle parties"—may exist under the political systems of Continental Europe; but the pressure of all our traditions, and of all our methods of Government, will be against the continued existence of such a party in this country. After a brief period of painful struggle against the inevitable, the Liberal party, if this is to be its character, will disappear, shedding one half of its members on the one side, and the other half on the other. That is the conclusion which the Labour party desires and is working for; and if Liberalism is now to be regarded merely as a compromise, and not as a positive faith, the Labour party is right in its aim, and the sooner the process is consummated, the sooner clarity will return to our politics.

It is the purpose of this book to show that this is a false conclusion, and that the three parties to which our political fortunes are henceforward committed do not stand to one another like three sections of the same straight line, with Liberalism in the central position, insensibly shading off into its neighbours; but that their relation is rather that of the three angles of a triangle, each definitely opposed to the other two, yet each linked with the other two, and having some points of sympathy with both.

So sharply defined are these three attitudes that it is almost possible to define each of them in a single word. The ideal of Conservatism is Stability, the ideal of Labourism is Equality, and the ideal of Liberalism is Liberty. And it needs little reflection to show that these ideals are essentially incompatible one with another. In particular, the devotee of Liberty will not accept the idea of Stability in a world where real freedom for all has not yet been realized; nor will he admit that Equality in any complete sense can be realized, or would bring happiness, among men who vary infinitely in their gifts of mind and will.

Conservatism stands, on the whole, as its name suggests, for the defence of things as they are, with only such changes as may be necessary for security. In this it is opposed both by Liberalism and by Labourism, which are alike dissatisfied with things as they are, and alike desire change, though in divergent directions.

Labourism stands, as its professed creed proclaims, for a radical reconstruction of human society as a whole, according to plans woven from the brain-stuff of theorists. It conceives of human society in the similitude of a building which can be demolished and rebuilt once you have agreed upon a building plan. In this it is opposed both by Liberalism and Conservatism : by Conservatism because it desires the minimum of change ; by Liberalism because it conceives of human society as a living and growing thing, which cannot with impunity be carved into totally new forms like the hapless creatures in Wells's *Island of Dr. Moreau*, but which is suffering from many maladies that need the attention of a skilled and patient doctor who will know how to call the laws of Nature to his aid.

Finally, Liberalism stands, as its name implies, for the progressive emancipation of all human individualities from the restraints which forbid the development of their full potentialities ; because it believes that individual character, energy and inventiveness are the mainspring of human progress. To this aim it finds obstacles both in Conservatism and in Labourism ; in Conservatism because it is chary of interfering with existing rights and privileges, which often form the chief restraints upon the full development of suppressed personalities ; in Labourism because it is apt to pin its faith to regimentation and mechanical organization, and believes in equality and uniformity more than in liberty and variety.

Between each two of these opposed creeds there are links of sympathy. Labourism and Conservatism are both instinctively authoritarian, and the extreme wings of both are prone to resort to force instead of persuasion. Liberalism and Labourism are linked by an instinctive dislike of entrenched privilege, and an instinctive sympathy with the under-dog. Liberalism and Conservatism are united in their distrust of mechanical reconstruction, and in their belief that private enterprise must, in the future as in the past, provide the main driving force in the economic sphere, though the Liberal takes a broader and the Conservative a narrower view of the modes and the spheres in which such enterprise should be encouraged to display itself.

Now our primary concern, in this book, is with the creed, the past achievements, and the future tasks of Liberalism. But that creed, and those achievements and tasks, stand forth all the more clearly by contrast with the two opposing standpoints; and it will therefore be helpful, before embarking upon our main theme, to dwell a little more fully upon the triangular antithesis which we have just described in very general terms. It would be possible to illustrate this antithesis in many spheres; to show how it would display itself in foreign policy, in practical administration, in local government, in education, in political organization. But the field in which the antithesis is most sharp is the field of social and industrial organization. Here, in truth, will be found, in the future, the main lines of demarcation between the three policies; and therefore, at the risk of anticipating in some degree what will be said later on these themes, we shall endeavour to define the attitudes of the three parties primarily in regard to the problems of social organization, so far as it is possible to do so in the nebulous condition of contemporary thought on these subjects.

III. CONSERVATISM AND LABOURISM

Conservatism stands for the defence of the existing economic order in all its main features. It will strive to uphold the existing rights and powers of land owners, mine owners, factory owners, financiers. There are, it is true, more generous elements among the Conservative party, who feel a certain uneasiness when they contemplate some aspects and consequences of the condition of industry to-day. But some of these are merely hereditary Conservatives, whose true place is either in the Liberal party or in the Labour party; whilst others instinctively hold a sort of feudal view of the relations of classes, and, while they desire that the workers should be humanely treated, hold that their well-being must depend upon the beneficence of the master-class, rather than upon law and established right. In any case, the dominant and controlling interests in the Conservative party are, and always will be, the powerful vested interests which see nothing gravely wrong in the present economic order. They stand for the defence of "private enterprise," but when they use that phrase, they think almost exclusively of the enterprise that is practised by the controlling interests in business, by the master-class; they do not stop to ask themselves whether the existing order gives full vent to the enterprise of men and women of every type, or whether it supplies the conditions which will enable and encourage every man to use his powers to the utmost, both for his own and the community's advantage. Moreover, there are in the Conservative party large elements which are continually tempted to trample down all movements of unrest or opposition, and to use force rather than persuasion as the easiest weapon for dealing with any sign of revolt against the established order. This temper is not at the moment predominant in Conservatism. But it is always present. It expresses itself in unbridled denunciation of trade unions and all their works, or even of the working class as a whole. It may at any moment get the upper hand, and persuade a Conservative government that "firm action" and "a fight to a finish" are the true remedies for industrial unrest.

Over against Conservatism stands the Labour party, whose declared aim is a complete and fundamental reconstruction of the whole existing economic order. It definitely intends to put an end to "private enterprise" as the driving force in our industrial system, and to substitute for it some form of organization of all industrial activity under the ownership of the community, and under the control either of the State or of the workers in each industry. True that when, at a bye-election in 1922, Mr. Arthur Henderson, the secretary of the party, indiscreetly blurted out the fact that his party aimed at abolishing "what is called private enterprise," there was an outcry of protest from many of his supporters. But Mr. Henderson was entirely right. He was expounding the central article of his party's creed; his critics were men who had been guilty of the intellectual dishonesty of joining the party without stopping to consider whether they accepted its creed. For the Labour party is definitely and unmistakably a Socialistic party. At a party conference at Nottingham in 1918, at which its organization was revised, it passed, *nemine contradicente*, a resolution declaring that its aim was "the nationalization of *all* the means of production, distribution and exchange"; and as this resolution has never been withdrawn or qualified, every adherent of the Labour party must be held to be committed to it. There are, no doubt, many thousands of members or supporters of the Labour party who have swallowed this formula without having grasped what it means—many who have joined the party out of sheer impatience with the evils of the existing order. And there are also many thousands more who give the party their allegiance merely because it is a class party, without having seriously analysed its doctrines. For a class party it quite definitely and predominantly is. It draws its strength mainly from the trade unions, and its funds almost wholly from trade union levies. A large part of its representation in parliament consists of trade union officials who feel themselves to be there not primarily for the purpose of representing their constituents, but primarily for the purpose of upholding the interests of the union which pays their expenses; and for many of these men the formulæ which their party has adopted have just as much, and just as little, meaning as the formula of Divine Right and Passive Obedience had for the Tory squires of the seventeenth century who ultimately drove out James II. But when all these qualifications are made, the Labour party remains definitely a Socialistic party, and its whole social and industrial policy, its attitude upon every proposal as it arises, must be coloured by its ultimate aims. Any project which would improve, and by improving strengthen, the system which rests upon private enterprise, must be suspiciously regarded by the sincere Socialist.

The Labour party is therefore pledged to a policy of wholesale demolition and reconstruction, but it has no clear view as to how the reconstruction is to be carried out. It has, indeed, definitely declared against Communism and the confiscation of all privately owned capital. The owners of capital are to be bought out, receiving government scrip at a fixed rate of interest in exchange for their holdings. This means that those of them who now render important services of management in return for their profits would cease to do so, and would have to be replaced by salaried officers. It also means that instead of receiving a high remuneration when trade is good, and a low remuneration when trade is bad, and thus bearing part of the brunt of bad trade, the owners of capital would, in the Socialist State, receive a steady rate of remuneration guaranteed by the State, whatever the condition of trade. And it further implies that the risk of trying out new ideas, which is now taken by private entrepreneurs, and often ends in the total loss of their capital, would have to be undertaken by the State, if it were undertaken at all; and as the capital which the State would have to invest in these enterprises would bear a permanent burden of interest whether they succeeded or failed, it follows that such ventures would very rarely be undertaken. These do not seem very happy devices for encouraging productive enterprise, increasing employment, and enlarging the nation's wealth; but they are the methods to which the Labour party is committed.

There is no sort of agreement among the prophets of the Labour party as to the mode in which nationalized industry is to be organized and controlled. Some—the State Socialists—advocate control by Government officials, checked by parliamentary ministers. Others—the Guild Socialists—urge that the body of workers in each industry should exercise control, choosing their own representatives to perform the highly expert and difficult duties of direction and management. Yet others suggest (as in the Coal Mines Bill proposed by the Labour party) a combination of these two methods. But, in whatever form, "democratic control" of industry is the accepted principle; and it is assumed that miscellaneous bodies of untrained electors or workpeople can safely be trusted to find, by means of the ballot, the persons most competent to perform highly skilled and expert work. Moreover, the persons thus selected are expected to perform their work with complete efficiency without being stimulated by the knowledge that they will profit by success and lose by failure. For it is an essential element in the ideals of the Labour party that what is called "the motive of gain" is to be banished and to be replaced by "the motive of service": even those who have to perform the dullest drudgery are no longer to be stimulated by the fear that if they don't work honestly they will be discharged, or by the hope that if they work hard they will get more pay; "the motive of service" is to be their all-sufficient stimulus. This aspiration has a very noble sound. But does it not overlook the fact that the motive of service to oneself and one's family is a perfectly legitimate one, not fairly expressed by the term "gain"? Does it not disregard the fact that in all honest work both the self-regarding and the altruistic motives are almost invariably present and that (especially in the higher types of work) the pride of doing one's job well, for its own sake, is often as powerful as either?

There is obviously an element of sentimentalism and unreality in the outlook of the Labour party. And it co-exists, in considerable sections of the party, with a passion of mere bitterness and hatred, which is not unnatural, but which is very unhealthy. Mazzini once said of Karl Marx that he distrusted him because "hatred outweighed love in his heart"; and the same judgment might be made upon many of the most active elements in the Labour party. Hate is a dangerous poison of the mind; it clouds the mental vision and forbids clear thinking. It leads easily to violence; and while the leaders of the Labour party and the bulk of their followers are anxiously constitutional, there are potent factors in the party which believe rather in brute force than in persuasion, and which are for ever driving towards violent methods, towards the use of Direct Action and the employment of compulsion by the interruption of necessary services, as a means of forcing the community to accept conclusions to which it cannot be brought by the legitimate processes of discussion and persuasion.

IV. THE LIBERAL ATTITUDE

If there is truth in our analysis of the normal attitudes of Conservatism and Labourism, it would seem that there is a real danger of an ugly class-war between the forces and ideas which they represent; a danger which would become very serious if these two parties were the only organized political forces in the country, arrayed in irreconcilable antagonism one against the other. The ugliness of class-war might indeed be qualified by moderation and good temper on both sides—qualities which can usually be counted upon in British public life. But for all that, class-warfare would become the outstanding and dominating fact of our politics.

Happily there is a third position possible—not a position intermediate between Conservatism and Labourism, but a third angle of the triangle, equally opposed to both, and it is in this third position that there is to be found the chief hope of a peaceful progression towards a happier order. Liberalism believes with the Labour party that there is much that is evil and unjust in our social order; but it believes that the vague and hazy projects of the Labour party would bring, not betterment, but confusion and impoverishment. It believes with Conservatism that "private enterprise" must be in the future, as it has been in the past, the mainspring of progress, and that to destroy "private enterprise" in the hope of producing social betterment is like taking the mainspring out of a watch in the hope of making it keep better time. But its diagnosis of the existing order is not that there is too much " private enterprise " (as the Labour party thinks), but that there is not nearly enough.

The conditions of to-day actually have the effect, in many ways, of inhibiting or restraining the " private enterprise " of multitudes of men. In many trades honest men have accepted the fundamentally immoral doctrine that it is right for them deliberately to do less than their best, lest their employers should reap undue profit from their activity; and schemes of profit-sharing or of payment by results are often rejected on the precise ground that they may tempt men to show " private enterprise," and to work hard for their own advantage. These strange conclusions are not the outcome of any superfluity of naughtiness on the part of the men who adopt them; they are in some degree the outcome of mistaken theories, but they are also part of an organized system of defence against certain recognized dangers and evils which undeniably exist; and they will not be abandoned until the evils which produce them are cured. We are, as yet, far indeed from having created conditions which will enable and encourage every man to make the most and the best of all his powers in freedom, for his own advantage and the community's at the same time. Yet until such conditions have been established it cannot be said that the system of society which depends upon " private enterprise " has had a fair trial. In the view of Liberalism it is the duty of the community to bring such conditions into existence; or, to put the same thing in the words of a great Liberal philosopher, T. H. Green, " it is the business of the State to maintain the conditions without which a free exercise of the human faculties is impossible."

That is, and that has always been, the task of Liberalism. We shall see in later chapters how much

—far more than is generally realized—Liberalism has achieved in this direction; we shall also see how much, and along what lines of work, still remains to be done. As fully as ever in the past, Liberalism stands for the abolition of restrictions upon individual freedom, which Conservatism defends; while Labourism stands for the imposition of what, in a Liberal view, would be new and dangerous restrictions upon freedom.

In short, while pinning its faith to the free enterprise of individuals as the motive-force of progress, Liberalism recognizes that the system of private enterprise, as it works to-day, is accompanied by, and is in some degree the cause of, certain grave evils which can only be remedied by the use of the organized power of society.

It will be our business to deal more fully later with these subjects; in the meanwhile it may suffice to enumerate three main defects of the existing order, against which Liberalism conceives it to be its duty to strive with all its force. The first is the maldistribution of wealth, the juxtaposition of extremes of riches and penury, and the fact that great accumulations of wealth are often gained by illegitimate and unsocial means. The second is the cruel insecurity which overhangs great masses of our people from childhood till death; the fear of an old age spent in the workhouse after a life of toil; the fear that even a brief spell of sickness may break up the home, and destroy the foundations of life; the continual fear of unemployment, due to movements of trade entirely beyond the sufferer's control. And the third, which has become more clearly realized and more sharply felt in proportion as our people have obtained education, is the humiliating feeling that working folk are treated as mere instruments of wealth-making, thrown aside when they are not wanted, and denied any share of control over the conditions in which they have to work, or any sense of citizenship in the industries to which their lives and strength are given. These are real and great evils which attend our existing social order. They are not necessary consequences of a system based upon private enterprise; indeed, as we have seen, they form in some ways a discouragement to private enterprise. They are the main causes of social unrest. And, provided that we can go on producing a sufficient volume of wealth to maintain our people in reasonable comfort, these evils are all capable of being cured. The responsibility of doing everything in its power to cure them is a responsibility which Liberalism accepts, as we shall later demonstrate.

It is needless to pursue the contrast between the spirit and attitude of the three parties into other fields, though it would be instructive to do so. But enough has perhaps been said to justify the main contention of this chapter, and to show that there are three distinct points of view in our politics, as definitely opposed to one another as the three angles of a triangle; and that the point of view of Liberalism is (to say the least) quite as necessary to the well-being of the community as either of its rivals. So long as this remains true, Liberalism will not be crushed out of existence. It has an inspiration as great as it ever possessed, and tasks lie before it which may well challenge the enthusiasm of its adherents.

CHAPTER II

A PRACTICABLE IDEAL

I. POLITICAL IDEALS

IT is easy enough to define political creeds in general terms—in words ending in *-ism* and *-tion*. But this is not enough for the plain man. He wants something clearer and more concrete. He knows well enough that we must advance step by step towards whatever goal we have set before us. But he feels that our steps must be wavering and uncertain unless we have some definable goal. And he not unreasonably expects that any political party which claims his allegiance will give him some sort of picture of the kind of society it aims at creating. A party which has a positive faith ought to be able to give some satisfaction to this demand.

The Conservative party, indeed, is under no obligation to meet this challenge. Many of its members believe in their hearts that the ideal state of society was in the past, and that the world is going from bad to worse; the most they hope for is to retard the rapidity of our descent to ruin. For many others the present is good enough—modified a little here and there, but not fundamentally altered; and this is the instinctive attitude of the great majority of Conservatives. Even the idealists of Conservatism (and there are such), while they recognize the existence of many evils, feel that stability and discipline are so essential to a healthy social system that they are always ready to resist "unsettling" proposals of change, and are suspicious of any drastic projects of reform.

Socialists, on the other hand, revel in sketching Utopias. They are always ready to give you a picture of a mechanically reconstructed society in which finality will have been attained, discontent will have been banished, and there will be nothing more to dream of or to hope for. They are, in truth, much more ready to do this than to give you any convincing account of the path by which their ideal is to be reached.

Can Liberalism do any better than the rival political creeds? Can it avoid, on the one hand, the blankness of the Conservative outlook, and on the other the unreality and the mechanical completeness of the Socialist vision? Can it describe a possible future state of society which could be developed out of the existing order, by the work and thought of imperfect and half-trained men such as we are, and by the use of such political machinery as we possess or can devise? Can it envisage an ideal which will not be in the clouds, but will take account of all the difficulties, national and international, by which we are surrounded?

In the nature of things Liberalism cannot give a very cock-sure or cut-and-dried description of its ideal society. It cannot do this, precisely because it believes in the infinite variety and the unpredictable capabilities of the human mind and will; because it holds that these unmeasured forces are the motive-power of progress; and because its fundamental conviction is that in proportion as these forces are released by an enlargement of real liberty, humanity will advance to unimagined victories. Its supreme aim is, and always has been, to create by co-operative effort such conditions as will make it possible for all men and women, and for all natural groups—nations, cities, villages, churches, parties, trade organizations, or voluntary associations—to make the most of their powers, and to strive after their ideals in freedom, so long as they do not invade the corresponding freedom of others. And no man may predict what would be the outcome of the activities which would thus be stimulated.

Who could have predicted, a hundred years ago, the political and social results which were to flow from the inventions of the nineteenth century—inventions which were made possible by the enlarged, though very imperfect, freedom and opportunity offered by that century to individual initiative and enterprise ? Who dare predict to-day the consequences which are likely to follow, not merely from new mechanical inventions, but from the new lines of investigation in psychology and other sciences upon which free inquiry is now embarking ? The one thing certain is that, if they are not interrupted by some cataclysm in which civilization will be ruined, they will transform the social as well as the material conditions of our world ; and he would be a bold man who would venture to foretell the state of human society even fifty years hence.

Nevertheless, it is possible for a Liberal to describe, in general terms, the kind of society that he desires to see brought into being. It will be a very different society from the rigid, static, regimented society which the Socialist imagines. It will be very different, also, from the society of to-day, with which the Conservative is so nearly content. But, unlike the Socialist State, it will have grown by a natural process out of the society we know, without any violent upheaval; and it will be linked with it by a continuity of tradition and of general character.

II. THE NATION AND ITS RELATIONS WITH OTHER NATIONS

To begin with, the ideal State of the Liberal will be a national State, with a distinctive national character. England will still be English and France French, and each people will take pride in its national characteristics; they will not have been merged in a featureless cosmopolitanism. Liberalism has always had a profound belief in the national spirit, and for this reason has always given eager sympathy to all legitimate demands for national freedom and unity. A nation is a great body of people who feel that they "belong together" because they are linked by a multitude of ties—ties of tradition, of language, of modes of thought and habits of life—which combine to create among them a real homogeneity; and wherever such ties exist, they provide the healthiest foundation for a State. It is only the homogeneity which nationhood creates that renders self-government workable among vast masses of men and women, or makes it possible for them to act as a community. The system of self-government has never worked well in any large State which was not organized upon a national basis, because majority rule is only tolerable when the majority is not sharply divided in sentiment from the minority. Moreover, it is the variety of the national types which have grown up within the civilization of Europe that has kept this civilization alive and progressive. For these reasons the Liberal feels no regret for the support which he and his predecessors have given to national movements in all parts of the world; he hopes for still further victories for this cause, as the national spirit takes root among diverse peoples and knits them into unity; and his ideal State must therefore be a national State, free from all external dictation in the management of its own concerns.

It has become fashionable to-day, among a number of facile and shallow thinkers, to condemn the national spirit as the source of international friction, and as a danger to the world's peace. Like any other great and beneficent force, the national spirit *can* be a danger when it gets out of hand. A river can be a danger, when it floods and desolates the plains which it usually enriches; fire can be a danger when it is uncontrolled, but it is also an essential source of light and warmth and power. It is as easy and as foolish to condemn the national spirit because of the harm which has sometimes resulted from it as it would be to demand the abolition of rivers and of fire because of the evil they have sometimes wrought. The national spirit is a potent force with which we cannot dispense in our labours for human well-being. But like other great forces it must somehow be restrained within the sphere in which it is helpful and creative.

The national State of the Liberal's ideal must not, therefore, be wholly uncontrolled, any more than the individual citizen must be wholly uncontrolled. Each needs to be restrained by Law, not only for the sake of others but for his or its own sake. The Liberal State must not exist in a condition of perpetual fear, wasting its substance in arming itself to the teeth against the possibility of attack by other States; nor must it be driven to seek for safety in an alliance with one group of States against another group, each group constantly watching its rivals suspiciously, and waiting for the tocsin of war. The Liberal wants his State to be really free; and fear is the enemy of freedom, war is its ruin, piled-up armaments devour the wealth whereby the material basis of freedom can be secured for the people.

The Liberal nation-State, therefore, will be linked with all the other civilized nations of the earth in a great League of Nations, which will put an end to the constant fear of war, relieve the peoples from the necessity of wasting their substance upon competitive armaments, and create the conditions wherein every nation will be able to make its distinctive contribution in freedom to the common stock of civilization. Through the League they will combine for many common purposes, and, in particular, for the settlement of their disputes by rational means. The councils of the League will be the arena in which all international relations will be determined, and there will be no secret bargainings or treaties outside its purview. Thus the Reign of Law will be extended from the relations between individuals to the relations between States. The Reign of Law is the foundation of liberty; and until it is established, no State, however powerful, can be really free, just as no individual can enjoy full liberty unless he is protected by Law against possible attacks by his neighbours, and against the beast in himself.

The League of Nations in the Liberal ideal will be genuinely a League—a banding together of equal partners for certain agreed purposes. It will not be a super-State. It will have no power of imposing its will upon its members, except in matters to which they have voluntarily pledged themselves; it will have no power of interfering in the internal concerns of its members, or dictating their form of government; it will have no power of levying taxes upon their citizens. It will not maintain an army capable of overawing any recalcitrant State, since the commander of such an army would have in his hands the means of making himself the despot of the world ; it will trust to the action of its member-States in fulfilment of their pledges, and to agreements for mutual defence among them which will require its endorsement and only become operative when the League so decrees. In the distant future the League may develop into something more than this, but, as far ahead as we can see, the States which are included within it must be in the fullest sense free States, masters of their own destinies—and all the more free because they are secure and at peace.

Under the shelter of the League, mutual suspicions and enmities between States will die down ; and one of the results of this, for which the Liberal hopes, should be that tariff-wars will fall as much out of fashion as military wars. In that event, unnecessary and artificial obstacles to the free intercourse of peoples will be thrown down ; and each nation will get that share of the world's trade to which it is entitled by the extent and character of its natural resources, and by the numbers, skill, honesty and enterprise of its people. The world will, we may hope, have learnt that all peoples are interdependent, that it is the prosperity of other nations and not their ruin which causes any nation to thrive, and that (in an industrial age) it is no longer possible for any nation, however great, to be self-sufficient. These are the principles upon which the Liberal doctrine of Free Trade has always rested. But even if other nations are so foolish as not to recognize these patent truths, the Liberal State will cling to complete freedom of interchange, and its markets will be open to all the world. By pursuing this policy undeviatingly it will make the greatest contribution in its power to the intercourse and amity of all peoples.

II. THE FELLOWSHIP OF THE BRITISH COMMONWEALTH

Besides its association with the other members of a world-wide league of olvilization, the Liberal Britain of the future will continue to be bound by more intimate ties to the great brotherhood of free nations which constitute the British Commonwealth. These ties will not be ties of sovereignty, in any but the most formal sense; they will not be ties of exclusive trade-agreements; they will not even be ties of common defence, except in so far as the Commonwealth may act as a unity in fulfilling its obligations under the League, for the League will have dispensed with the necessity of any elaborate defence organization. They will be ties of mutual understanding, arising from a common pride in the same institutions of freedom, and in the same heritage of culture and thought. They will lead to an incessant interchange of scholars, thinkers, and statesmen, and to fruitful mutual contributions of social and political experiment; and they will make easier the unforced, steady and necessary transfer of population from the crowded homeland to the young and half-empty lands which, in spite of distance, will still be home-like to the immigrant.

Again, even when the Liberal ideal has been realized, it is probable that Britain will not have ceased to play the part of a bringer of civilization to the backward peoples of the world. There will be large areas inhabited by such peoples which will be in a state of political dependence upon her; and many young Englishmen will find their life-tasks in the administration of these regions, in the teaching of their peoples, and in the development of their economic resources. Undeniably there is danger in these tasks; the government of a lower by a higher race may easily become a tyranny, and the development of economic resources may be, and often has been, the cover for a brutal exploitation. Fearing these ills, there are many men of Liberal mind who denounce the whole system whereby backward peoples are brought under civilized control; they demand that we should forswear what is called imperialism, and leave the primitive peoples to enjoy the blessings of "self-determination." But this has never been the accepted Liberal view. For primitive peoples "self-determination" means stagnation, even if they could be left alone—they have enjoyed this doubtful boon for untold centuries, and it has not availed to raise them out of barbarism. And since, in the restless modern world, it is impossible that they should be left undisturbed, it is best that they should be brought under the responsible tutelage of a civilized government. To exercise this tutelage is part of the duty of free and advanced communities; it offers the only means of progress for the backward peoples, the only means whereby the Reign of Law and the liberty which it creates can be extended to them; and to abandon this task because it has sometimes been ill-performed is a cowardly abnegation of responsibility.

But the control of a Liberal State over primitive subjects will not be a mere brutal domination, exploiting them for the benefit of the ruling race. The Liberal State will, in this relation, regard itself as a trustee—a trustee for its simple subjects on the one hand, and for the civilized world on the other; and its trusteeship will henceforward be subject to the watchful criticism of the world, with the League of Nations as its organ.

It will ensure that its agents take an exalted view of their duties, and regard their task as that of leading primitive peoples out of barbarism into civilization, not interfering unnecessarily with their customs or overriding their rights, but helping them to manage their own affairs, protecting them against injustice on the part of immigrant white men, and stamping out slavery and barbarities of many kinds. Nor will these dependent lands be treated as an exclusive trade reserve for the merchants of the mistress-State. Equal access will be given (as it has long been given) to the traders of all nations; and the fairness with which this trust on behalf of civilization is performed will be tested by submission to the frank and open criticism of the other nations in the League.

These relations with the self-governing Dominions, and with the backward peoples, will not involve any sudden departure from the principles of British Imperial policy. They will be the natural development of the policy which Liberalism has steadfastly pursued for a century past, and which has transformed the character of the British Empire, and made the word "empire," with its suggestions of military domination, no longer a satisfactory description of this amazing fellowship of peoples. The Liberal State will not only enjoy freedom itself; it will be—as indeed it has been in the past—the means of extending freedom to other peoples on as ample a scale as they are capable of enjoying.

Thus the nation-State of the Liberal ideal will not by any means have lost its character by being merged in a vague universal State; but neither will it be an isolated unit. It will be linked by a variety of ties with all the peoples of the earth, and more intimately with that great group of peoples—more than one-quarter of the world's population—whom the accidents of history, or a community of race, speech and tradition, have brought into peaceful fellowship and co-operation with one another in the British Commonwealth. These relations will profoundly affect the conditions of life within the nation-State itself. And they will place in its hands, in conjunction with its kindred nations, the opportunity and the responsibility of wielding a great influence upon the course of world-events. Whatever other blunders we may be guilty of, we must never think of the Liberal State as if it were an isolated unit whose organization can be planned without reference to the complex world-society of which it is a member. That is a blunder to which the dreamers of Socialism are but too prone.

IV. DEMOCRACY, SELF-GOVERNMENT, VARIETY

But it is with the character and organization of the British State itself that the Liberal ideal is especially concerned; and to that we must next turn, first sketching its main characteristics in general terms, and then dealing, a little more fully, with the methods by which these characteristics are to be determined.

Freedom will be its supreme characteristic. Its glory will be that it has succeeded, by co-operative effort, in creating such conditions of life that every man can feel he has a real opportunity of making the most of his powers, and that (so far as the circumstances of organized social life permit) he is free to do, in his own way, whatever he is fit for and thinks right, provided that his action does not interfere with the corresponding liberty of his neighbours. But freedom has, as its correlative, responsibility. In the Liberal State every citizen, being assured by the community of the minimum conditions necessary for freedom, will know that beyond this minimum he is responsible for his own well-being and for that of his family; and he will know, also, that in his degree he is responsible for the well-being of the community as a whole.

Because it is a free society, the Liberal State will also be a democratic and a self-governing society. These two terms "democratic" and "self-governing" are not mere synonyms. It is possible to imagine a society which could correctly be described as a democracy, wherein an organized majority, consisting perhaps exclusively of citizens of a single class or type, and these possibly not the wisest or the best informed, might exercise a tyrannical sway over a helpless minority. Such a society, though it would be a democracy, would not be in any genuine sense either free or self-governing; for the minority would have no real freedom, and they would in no sense possess the right of governing themselves. The Liberal State will not be democratic in this sense; it will be democratic in the sense that every citizen will feel he has an effective share in the responsibility for common affairs, and that his voice counts. Nor will the democratic character of the Liberal State mean that in it an equal value and influence belong to each individual; but rather that a man's value and influence are determined by what he is and what he does, not by what he possesses, or by what his grandfather did, or by the power wielded by any organized group of which he may be a member.

Again, when we say that the Liberal State will be a self-governing society, we do not mean merely that every citizen will have the right, once in five years, of marking a cross upon a ballot-paper in favour of one of two or three candidates, none of whom may inspire his confidence, with the knowledge that his vote will count for nothing at all unless it happens to be given to the candidate who has the luck to obtain a majority. So far as national politics are concerned, this is as far as we have yet got in the organization of self-government; and it is not very far. In the Liberal State self-government will mean much more than this. It will mean that in the election of the national Parliament every clearly defined body of opinion will be assured of a representation equivalent to its numerical strength, so that the mind of the nation as a whole will be fairly represented in the criticism and control of the national government, and every citizen will feel that his voice has had some weight. It will mean that (by devolution and in other ways) the functions of Parliament, which are now so immense that they cannot be performed, will be brought within practicable dimensions, so that the unchecked authority now largely wielded by cabinets and bureaucratic departments will be brought under effective review. It will mean that the British tradition of local self-government, which is stronger and healthier than that of any other country, will be yet more strengthened, so that at every stage—in the great region with its devolutionary assembly, in the county or the borough, in the district, in the village—it will be possible for the more able and public-spirited citizens to take an active part, and for the mass of citizens (especially in the lower stages) to check the behaviour of their representatives, in the conduct of common affairs. It will mean that spontaneous or voluntary organizations for common ends will be encouraged and aided, so long as their activity does not conflict with the general good. It will mean that in industrial and other affairs the interests concerned will be left so far as possible to regulate their own concerns under the supervision and authority of the State, instead of having their conditions of work dictated to them. And, finally, it will mean that at every stage the functions of government will be kept within the limits that are really necessary for the common good, so as to leave as large a sphere as possible for individual self-government, the importance of which we are a little too apt to forget.

The sphere of common regulation in the Liberal State will be a wide one, and its tendency will be to widen as society becomes more complex; but so far as possible the function of regulation will be entrusted to those who are most immediately concerned, instead of being exercised by small groups of politicians and officials in a highly centralized system. This is what the Liberal means by a self-governing society: not a society in which the organizers of an artificial majority, whose followers seldom understand the complex questions brought before them, exercise an arbitrary and dictatorial sway over the whole sphere of communal life, and invade, as and when they think fit, the freedom of action of the individual; but a society in which all common interests, and only common interests, are regulated by the groups or sections of the community which are most immediately concerned, subject to the supreme controlling power of Parliament, which is the mouthpiece of the community as a whole. The general description which we have here attempted to give may seem a little abstract and theoretical, but its significance will become more apparent when we come to look more closely at some special aspects of the social organization of the Liberal State.

But our free Liberal State will not only be democratic and self-governing, it will also be a very varied society, far more varied and interesting than that of to-day; for variety is the necessary corollary of liberty. There will be no hidebound regimentation of the citizens, and no attempt to establish an artificial equality among men who are naturally unequal and different. The only forms of equality which it will pursue will be equality before the law, and equality of opportunities for all citizens to make the most of their varying powers.

There will be differences of class, but they will not be hereditary, nor will there be any sharp cleavage between the classes; for the class to which a man will belong will not be fixed by any accident of birth (except in so far as a good breed always tells), but by each man's character and ability. There will be rich men and poor men, for the man who has the gifts that make for material success will be encouraged to use them, so long as he does not employ them in anti-social ways. But there will be no hopeless mass of sordid destitution, for the community will have attained the Liberal ideal of fixing, "not a high-water mark beyond which no man may rise, but a low-water mark below which no man will be allowed to fall."[1] And there will be no vast accumulations of inherited wealth to be idly enjoyed; for though rich men will be allowed and encouraged to make ample provision for their children and to give them a good start in life (since this is one of the most honourable incentives to effort and thrift), they will not be permitted to bequeath vast wealth, and all the power it wields, to any individual. A man may justly inherit from his father a reasonable competence which will relieve him from anxiety and leave him free to pursue, if he so desires, an unremunerative calling; but that is a different thing from inheriting the irresponsible power over his fellows which great wealth gives. There will thus be a leisured class, but it will not be very rich; and a leisured class has great social value except

[1] This phrase is Lady Bonham Carter's.

when it is tempted by great riches to waste itself in lavish living. Again, there will be many who will pursue the exciting and inspiring adventures of the intellectual life, finding their reward not often in money, but in the fascination of their work; and there will be great numbers whose working hours (not unduly long) will necessarily be spent in routine drudgery. There will be, as now, a small class who will initiate, direct, and issue orders, and a huge class who will be content to receive orders; but the orders will not be merely arbitrary, since those who have to obey them will be consulted as to their fairness, in all reasonable ways; nor will those who issue orders be able to wield any arbitrary power over the lives of those who accept them. All these varied classes will inevitably be differentiated from one another, and men will tend to find companionship mainly among those of their own type. In that sense class distinctions will survive. But there will be no sharp cleavage between the classes, for the passage from class to class in successive generations, or even within the same lifetime, will be of such common occurrence that any real cleavage will be impossible.

V. THE FUNDAMENTAL CONDITIONS OF FREEDOM—HEALTH AND EDUCATION

The description of the Liberal State which is set forth in the foregoing pages is couched in very general terms, and it cannot be convincing until these have been given greater concreteness. All very well to say that the Liberal State will be a free State in which all men will be able to make the most of their powers. But before this promise can be made to seem realizable, we must be able to give answers to two questions.

The first is the question how the citizens of the Liberal State will be enabled to obtain that control of their own powers which they cannot obtain by their own unaided efforts, and without which they cannot use such opportunities as may be opened to them ; for it is very obvious that in the conditions of to-day it is difficult, if not impossible, for great numbers of our citizens to obtain effective control of their own powers.

The second question is even more important. Given that the citizen has been enabled to realize his own capacities, how will it be ensured that both he himself and the community will genuinely profit by his exercising them to the utmost, and how will he be protected against the sense of insecurity in regard to the very foundations of his life, which, more than anything else, undermines the sense that a man is a free agent ? Some degree of security is a necessary foundation of liberty. Even in the earliest stages of civilization, it is only when the State has given some security against incessant danger to life and limb that liberty in any real sense begins to exist. And the insecurity which haunts the lives of a great part of our people to-day is not only the greatest evil of our industrial system, it forbids those who suffer from it to feel that they are fully free men : they are the chained slaves of circumstances over which they have no control. More than anything else, the feeling that this is so prevents them from wholeheartedly putting forth their strength in their work.

These two questions bring us to fundamentals. It is in the attempt to find a solution for them that the Socialist has been drawn on to devise an elaborate mechanical system which would in fact destroy freedom instead of creating it. And unless Liberalism can give answers to these questions, its ideal of freedom must remain a thing of mere words. These questions do, indeed, raise tremendous issues. The first asks what the community will do to help the individual to realize his own manhood. The second asks how the machinery of production can be organized so as to yield justice; and it can only be answered by a description of the way in which the whole economic system should be organized. In other words, we have to consider what will be the material basis of the freedom which is to be the chief characteristic of the Liberal State.

The State will assume the responsibility for ensuring that all citizens, and especially the young, enjoy the conditions necessary for physical health, and also that they are provided with the training needed to discover and to develop their mental powers. This is not only necessary as a means to freedom, it is a matter of sane public economy, since the physical and mental powers of the citizens are the nation's most valuable asset. Nor will the assumption of this responsibility be any new thing for Liberalism. Already, in fact, this responsibility has been accepted, though it is not yet adequately fulfilled; and it was Liberalism which accepted it, when, during its long ascendancy in the nineteenth century, it created a national system of education and a national organization for public health.

A vast deal remains to be done ere the conditions necessary for the breeding of a physically healthy people will have been secured. Slums must be cleared away; the foulness of smoke must be banished (as it can be banished) from urban areas; towns must be intelligently planned and provided with abundant open spaces; healthy houses must be provided in sufficient abundance for the whole population; competent medical advice must be available for everybody;

hospitals of many types must be numerous enough to meet all needs. Much of this work can only be done, as it is done to-day, by communal action. In regard to the rest, communal action may be necessary to supplement private enterprise, and must in any case be brought into play to regulate it. Liberal policy would dictate that wherever the necessary work can be effectively done by private enterprise, it should be left to private enterprise, but that the community should define the standards of adequacy which private enterprise must satisfy, and should fill any gaps which private enterprise leaves unfilled.

Thus, in the provision of houses, private builders or co-operative building guilds (provided they have to observe sufficiently stringent rules) are likely to show more ingenuity in catering for varied tastes, and to be more economical, than any public department; but it is the business of a public authority to see that building is carried on in accordance with a sound town-plan, that proper sanitary provisions are made, that the houses are honestly and solidly built, and that they have sufficient light and air. Thanks to the work of the local authorities which were established by Liberal legislation, and thanks to the powers with which they have been endowed and the duties which have been imposed upon them, we have already made substantial progress in this direction. These powers will be enlarged, especially in regard to the use and acquisition of land, and these duties will be more courageously undertaken; and in the Liberal State of the future every citizen will be assured of the conditions which make for physical health.

The importance of the services which the community must render to the individual citizen is even greater in the sphere of education than in the sphere of health. Here also the acceptance of communal responsibility has been mainly due to Liberal policy. Here also much has already been achieved. But here also a vast deal remains to be done ere the Liberal ideal of enabling every citizen to obtain a sufficient mastery of his own powers can be achieved. Classes must be reduced to a size which will make real teaching possible; the noble profession of the teacher must be made sufficiently dignified and attractive to draw into its service an army of men and women of the right types; physical, manual, and æsthetic training must be added to mere book-learning; every child of ability must be assured of obtaining the highest training which it can profitably absorb; and, since in many cases intellectual interests develop tardily, there must be a generous system of adult or adolescent education available for all who desire it.

All these things Liberal policy demands, as a condition precedent to the creation of a fully free community. But there is another thing which it equally demands. The English system of education has been very rapidly built up, mainly under the control of public authorities. For that reason it has tended, in an alarming degree, to assume the shape of a vast standardizing machine, which tends to obliterate individuality, and to turn out everybody to a pattern. Public authorities and their officials, central and local, are apt to distrust variations from the normal; they prefer uniformity because it is easily measured and tested; and, owing to their natural tendency to magnify their own functions, they are prone to leave little freedom to the individual school, and to show little trust in the teacher. Yet the function of training individual minds is, or ought to be, of all things the most individual. Here, if anywhere, the Liberal must feel that freedom and variety are supremely needful. They can only be attained if every encouragement is given to individual inspiration, and to voluntary effort. In the Liberal State not only will schools (and still more universities) be assured of the maximum practicable degree of autonomy, even when they are provided by public authorities, in order that they may develop distinct characteristics of their own; but all spontaneous movements of educational experiment will be welcomed and encouraged, and every qualified man, or group of men, who may be ready to start schools of distinctive types will be recognized, and will receive public aid, in proportion to the number of children they train, so long as they fulfil the broad requirements as to staff, equipment and standards of work which may be defined as universally necessary in the grade of work they undertake. In this, as in other spheres, Liberalism must desire to foster not uniformity but the utmost possible variety and elasticity of method.

The conditions necessary for physical health—the means for training one's mental powers to the furthest extent to which this training can usefully be carried under the formal discipline of the school—these are the preliminary conditions of a free life with which every citizen will be equipped in the Liberal State; and it will be a healthy people, possessed of the keys of knowledge, which will be called upon to enjoy the privileges, and to meet the responsibilities, of freedom.

VI. THE CONDITIONS OF ECONOMIC PROSPERITY

We have next to consider the economic structure of the Liberal State. This is the most difficult and the most vital part of our problem. Unless we can see our way clear in this field, it is useless to talk about the securing of a larger liberty; for liberty must rest upon a sound economic basis. And it is here that the Liberal ideal will find itself most sharply in conflict with its rivals.

There are certain basic realities of which any ideal must take cognizance; and it is the chief weakness of the Socialist scheme that it largely forgets or disregards these. The first of these stubborn facts is the fact that we are not dealing with an isolated society, but with one which is dependent for its very existence upon its relations with the rest of the world. We have to devise a healthy economic system for a dense population in a small island which cannot support itself from its own resources, but must buy the bulk of its food and of the raw materials of its industry from other peoples. It can only do so if it can produce commodities so attractive, so cheap and so abundant that they will find ready purchasers in every part of the world. The second stubborn fact is the fact that this society no longer possesses the superiority in coal and iron, or the marked advantage in mechanical devices, which brought it wealth and trading supremacy during the nineteenth century. It has to face acute and intelligent competition, and it is handicapped by the burdens of the war. This difficulty can only be solved by giving every possible stimulus to initiative and enterprise, by ensuring that we shall all work our hardest, and by avoiding the waste of friction and conflict. The third stubborn fact is that if we are to succeed we must every year set apart a large proportion of the wealth we create—perhaps as much as one-fifth or one-sixth of the total—to be used as capital for the renewal and improvement of our productive machinery. This is as necessary as it is that the farmer should annually set apart a proportion of his crop for seed. It can only be done if every possible incentive is provided to encourage saving and investment. To give the freest possible vent to every healthy form of enterprise—to create such conditions of work that every man, in every grade of industry, will feel impelled to work his hardest—to diffuse as widely as possible the habits of thrift by making it obviously worth while—these are the only ways in which a society, placed as ours is to-day, can hope to extricate itself from its difficulties.

In the ideal Liberal State our dependence upon foreign supplies, and our incapacity to feed ourselves, will have been qualified in some degree by a revival of agriculture, by the cultivation of forests which will give us a home-grown supply of timber, and by the re-population of the deserted countryside. The revival of agriculture (in so far as it is possible) will not be brought about by means of a protective tariff, which increases the cost of living of the whole community for the advantage not only of the actual cultivator but of the land-owner. Nor will it be effected by means of direct subsidies to the farmer, which bring with them a vexatious and often mischievous interference by the State (as the granter of the subsidies) with the farmer's freedom of action in tilling his land: dictation of this kind by government departments, even if it is guided by knowledge, is always apt to do harm, because the farmer who needs such control is, *ex hypothesi*, unlikely to know how to carry out his instructions, while the farmer who does not need it is sure to know the potentialities of his land better than any government department. Agricultural revival, if it is to come at all, will be brought about by the Liberal device of giving free play to enterprise, and creating the conditions which will encourage and help it: by amending the land system so as to make access to land more easy and tenure more secure, and so as to discourage the use of land for purposes of mere sport or social ostentation; by providing a just method of fixing rents and a fair apportionment of the public burdens which land has to bear; by strengthening the position of the peasant, ensuring him fair wages, and opening to his ambition the prospect of attaining first a small holding, and then a farm of his own, if he deserves it; by creating a system of banks which will make working capital available for men of character and industry; by encouraging in every possible way the practice of co-operation in buying, in selling, and in the use of efficient machinery, which has worked marvels in other countries; by carrying on incessant research on soils and the crops appropriate to them, and making the results available in an intelligible form.

But when all has been done that can be done in this field, we shall still be dependent upon our export trade; and our hopes of prosperity, and of making freedom more real, will still depend upon the extent to which we can stimulate universal thrift and universal hard work, and upon giving the freest vent to healthy enterprise.

For the provision of the capital necessary for the conduct of industry we have hitherto trusted largely (though not mainly) to a system whereunder a disproportionately large amount of the total wealth created passed into the hands of a few men, who, enjoying larger incomes than they could spend, found it easy to set apart considerable blocks of their wealth for capital purposes. This system, though it was better for the community than the methods of Bolshevik Russia, which practically forbade the creation of capital and therefore ruined the community, was (and is) an unhealthy system. It gave (and gives) a dangerous power to the fortunate few, and it is obviously unjust to the many. The Liberal ideal desires to substitute for this system one under which almost everybody would create and own capital, whether on a large or a small scale, just as almost everybody would work. But in order that this ideal may be realized two things are necessary. One is that it should be possible for men to earn, by extra effort, a real margin beyond subsistence; and this depends upon the way in which the proceeds of industry are distributed. The other condition is that there must be a reasonable security ere saving becomes advantageous. There must be security that what a man saves will be his own, at his free disposal, and not liable to arbitrary confiscation. But there must be more than this. There must be a reasonable security of livelihood. When a man feels that through circumstances which he cannot control the very foundations of his economic life may suddenly be destroyed, the small savings he can make are apt to seem not worth making: "let us eat and drink, for to-morrow we die." A reasonable security of livelihood is therefore as necessary to encourage thrift as it is to make freedom real.

As for the wholehearted and zealous work which is the second necessity for national prosperity, that is deterred, among great masses of our people, by two considerations, both of which have some real justification. In the first place, men feel that any extra effort they may put forth will redound only to the advantage of the rich master-class. In the second place, haunted by the spectre of unemployment, they believe that extra effort on their own part may have the effect of depriving some of their comrades of the means of livelihood. This is, of course, a wholly fallacious idea, though it is also a generous idea. If two men have to be engaged to do work that one could do, the resultant product must be more costly; it may be so much more costly that it will not find purchasers, and in that case both men will be thrown out of work, and the whole community will be impoverished. These two ideas—which are the cause of all the devices for restriction of output that hamper our trade—must be faced and removed. They can only be removed by an industrial system which on the one hand not only ensures that every man will reap a fair reward for extra effort, but also gives to him or his representatives access to trustworthy knowledge about the working of the industry such as will show that this happens; while, on the other hand, the system must ensure to all honest workers a reasonable security such as will satisfy them that those who are thrown into the reserve of the industrial army by some sudden change of markets are not left to drift. Security is essential as a condition of steady and honest work, just as it is essential as a means of encouraging thrift and making freedom real.

In the Liberal State these essential conditions for the encouragement of thrift and energetic work in all classes of the community will be realized, as we shall presently see. But they will not be realized (as Socialism would strive to realize them) in such a way as to cripple and destroy the third and greatest of the conditions of prosperity—the giving of a free vent to individual enterprise. The men of courage, originality and initiative, who are the natural leaders of a progressive society, must be left free to win and wield the leadership which belongs to them, in the economic sphere as in all others. Subject to such regulations and restraints as the community may impose, every man with a new idea must be free to develop it in his own way; every man who has capital at his disposal must be free to risk it upon any legitimate enterprise, and must be encouraged to do so by the prospect of making profits which will counterbalance the risk of loss ; every man who has confidence in his own skill in gauging the requirements of a market and in his own powers of organization must be free to test his powers, taking the risk and responsibility of leadership with its advantages. It is the business of the community to ensure that these activities are kept within proper limits by a sound system of commercial law. It is also the business of the community to ensure that the workers whom these leaders engage to carry on their enterprises are assured of fair treatment—of a just reward for their effort, and of a reasonable security not dependent upon the success or failure of the entrepreneur who engages them. But, subject to these conditions, the utmost freedom for private enterprise must continue to be, as it has been in the past, the driving-wheel of our economic order ; and those who prove their fitness for leadership must be able to enjoy the prerogatives of leadership.

Of the three broad conditions which we have laid down, the first two—the better distribution of the product of industry, and the provision of adequate security for the worker—cover the points at which Liberalism is most likely to come to conflict within Conservatism ; the third—the encouragement of private enterprise—covers the points on which Liberalism will necessarily come into conflict with Socialist Labourism.

VII. LIBERALISM AND CAPITALISM

It follows from what has been already said that while there will be a great variety of industrial method and organization in the Liberal State, the actual conduct and direction of most industrial concerns—the decision as to what is to be made, how it is to be made, and how it is to be marketed—will be mainly in the hands of entrepreneurs and directors like those of to-day—men who win their positions by their own achievements. The chief difference will be that they will have to work under conditions designed to secure the various safeguards for the worker set forth above. To these we shall have to return. Meantime something needs to be said about the working of the system of private enterprise as it would be in the Liberal State.

There will be a multitude of small private firms, especially in the less developed industries, for in some spheres small firms are most active in the working out of new methods. There will be a multitude of large and small limited liability companies, whose shares will be held by a vast army of investors drawn from all classes, including their own employees; but these companies will have to work under a far stricter system of Company Law than that of to-day—a system designed to guard against financial trickery, to prevent dishonest flotations, and to secure a much higher degree of publicity about their transactions than is now required. And there will be great trusts, or combines under working agreements, amounting in some cases to monopolies in certain fields. The Liberal State will not attempt to forbid such developments, which often lead to increased efficiency and economy. But it will take drastic measures to guard against the two great dangers which may spring from them—the danger that they may, by unfair competition, crush out promising new developments which might threaten their monopoly; and the danger that they may use their monopolist power to plunder the public. These are temptations which beset all monopolist concerns—and none more than government or municipal concerns, such as the Socialist theory favours. Free trade forms a partial safeguard against the danger of monopoly, since it exposes it to foreign competition even when home competition is ineffective. But the chief weapon which the Liberal State will adopt against these dangers will be a demand by law for full and detailed publicity as to the costings, earnings and spendings of such concerns—a method which has long since been adopted in the case of the railways. And it will hold in reserve the power of fixing prices for the commodities controlled by trusts, just as, ever since 1844, Government has reserved the power of fixing railway rates and fares. These powers, firmly and wisely applied, will safeguard the community against the dangers of trusts while allowing it to profit by the increased efficiency and economy which they often bring about.

Private firms—limited companies—trusts and combines—these may seem to reproduce completely the structure of what is called "capitalist" society. Will the Liberal State, then, be correctly described as a "capitalistic" State? The answer to this question depends upon the sense in which the questioner employs the much-abused term "capitalism."

Capitalism may in one sense be defined as a system wherein the capital invested in industry is (*a*) owned by the private individuals whose saving has created it, and (*b*) used for such purposes as its owners may desire. The first of these two conditions is repudiated by Communism, which does not allow anyone to own, or to draw interest from, his own savings. The second condition is repudiated by other forms of Socialism, which allow those who have saved to draw interest on their savings, but insist that they must be lent only to Government, and reserve to some public authority the power of deciding for what purposes they are to be used. On this definition the Liberal State would be, quite clearly, a capitalistic society; for we hold it to be essential not only that the man who saves should own his savings, but that he should be entitled to invest them as he thinks best —if in venturesome and novel experiments, so much the better for the community. One of the chief dangers of the Socialist scheme is that, if all capital were controlled by the State, venturesome experiments would seldom be undertaken; and if they were undertaken, the capital spent on experiments that failed would remain a permanent burden on which the community would have to pay interest to those who had provided it, whereas, under the existing system, it is wiped out as dead loss.

But there is another definition of Capitalism, whereby it means a system in which industry is entirely controlled by the owners of the capital invested in it, and is conducted exclusively for their advantage. In this sense the word does not accurately describe even the existing economic order, and it would be still less appropriate to the Liberal State of the future. And this for two distinct reasons: in the first place, because the Liberal State will include many industrial concerns which will not be in any sense or degree controlled by the owners of the capital employed in them; and in the second place, because even in those concerns in which private enterprise will be most unfettered, the owners of capital will by no means exercise an undivided control. Let us consider in order these two modes in which the capitalistic character of the Liberal State will be qualified.

There will be many forms of industrial organization in the Liberal State besides pure private enterprise;

no such uniformity of type will exist in it as the Socialist theory involves.

(1) Already, in the business of retail distribution, there has been an immense development of the co-operative system, wherein the supreme control is exercised by the consumer, not by the owner of capital. Liberalism has always supported and believed in this form of organization for the purposes to which it is appropriate. It will certainly grow; and it will be largely extended to both buying and selling in agriculture and other industries, which will thus be saved from paying excessive toll to middlemen.

(2) There will be a substantial development also of the form of co-operative production exemplified by the Building Guild and other bodies of the same type. This form of organization is probably only applicable to a limited number of industries, and it might lead to a mischievous exploitation of the public if it ever succeeded in achieving a monopolist control of any industry. But, short of this, it is to be welcomed and encouraged in the fullest degree, as affording a means whereby the worker can feel his own responsibility for, and partnership in, the work in which he plays a part. Liberalism will study and help experiments of this order with the warmest sympathy, and they will have their place in the variegated texture of the Liberal State.

(3) Even now municipalities carry on great undertakings which are entirely owned and controlled by the community. These undertakings (tramways, water, gas, electricity, and the like) are almost all of the nature of "public utilities," or essential public services which are necessarily of a monopolist character. Beyond a doubt they will be further extended. It may be noted that their employees and those of the co-operative societies require protection against insecurity or

unfairness every whit as much as the employees of private enterprise. The mere fact that an industrial concern is publicly owned does not cure the evils of which the workers complain.

(4) For the management of public utilities of another kind there already exist various public trusts, such as the Mersey Docks and Harbour Board, or the Port of London Authority, which do not work for a profit and are directed by representative controlling bodies. It may safely be assumed that this method of organization will be widely employed in the Liberal State for purposes to which it is appropriate.

(5) There are certain great public services of primary importance, such as the Post Office, the Telegraphs, the Telephones, and the construction of warships and armaments, which are wholly or partly under the direct ownership and control of the State, being managed by public officials under the direction of a political minister responsible to Parliament. This is the mode of organization which the State Socialists desire to extend to the whole sphere of industry. And there are certain vital public services, notably the railway system, which not only Socialists but many Liberals would be ready to bring under public ownership and control, not because they have any theoretical preference for public control, but because these services are essentially monopolistic in character and therefore need to be regulated.

Even in these cases, however, most Liberals have a profound distrust of the method of nationalization, not through any tenderness for the rights of existing owners, but because they feel that government control is open to some very grave defects. It may be laid down as a Liberal principle that the function of the State in regard to industry is to regulate the conditions under which it is carried on, with a view to safeguarding the interests of the community, rather than to carry it on itself; and the combination of regulation and direct control in the same authority is open to many criticisms. Nor is this the only objection to the conduct of an industry by Government. The way in which public officials are appointed and paid, and the secure tenure by which they hold their offices, are appropriate for regulative and quasi-judicial functions, but not for creative or productive functions, because they lead to undue formalism and delay. The exercise of supreme control by a political minister who usually has no special knowledge of his work, and who may, even if he is efficient, suddenly lose his office for reasons totally unconnected with his official functions, does not make for efficiency. Parliament is not a well-constituted body to criticize and review the working of vast organizations such as the Post Office or the railway system, and is in any case much too fully occupied to take such duties seriously. All these are grave objections to the direct control of great industrial undertakings by the ordinary machinery of Government. But there are yet graver objections. It is undesirable that the State should be made an immediate party in industrial disputes; it ought to stand outside of such disputes, as an impartial dealer of justice. But when any dispute arises between a department like the Post Office and its employees, the State is inevitably made a party; there is no satisfactory appeal beyond it; and the employees are taught to regard the State as their oppressor. And, finally, it is undesirable that large masses of work-people should be put in a position in which they can use their political power for the purpose of directly influencing their wages and conditions of labour, as they are bound to do when they become the direct employees of the State. Few candidates for Parliament would be able to resist the combined pressure of postmen and railway servants if these were brought to bear upon them in an election. And this brings the danger that elections may be decided, not on the great issues of national policy, which ought to determine them, but upon details affecting particular industries.

These considerations are conclusive against the direct control of great industrial undertakings by the ordinary machinery of government. But they do not exclude the possibility of another form of public control, which would be free from these dangers. If the telephones or the railways were placed under the control of a Public Trust constituted by Act of Parliament, exercising under the terms of the Act a large measure of independence, and not liable to continual political interferences, they would be more efficiently managed than by a government department of the ordinary type; Parliament would be relieved of a duty which it cannot properly perform; the State would be left to its true function of regulating rather than conducting industry; and yet, at the same time, the ultimate control would lie with the community, since Parliament could at any time revise the terms of the Acts by which these trusts were set up. In the ideal Liberal State essential national services, which are necessarily monopolistic in character, such as the telephones or the railways, will probably be withdrawn from the sphere of private enterprise and brought under public control. But they will not be managed by a government department and a political minister. They will be managed by powerful public bodies specially constituted for the purpose, and deriving their authority from Acts of Parliament, which will define the principles on which their work is to be conducted.

(6) There are certain other great industries which, while they cannot quite be described as essential national services, are nevertheless of basic importance for other industries. These are especially the industries concerned with the supply of power—coal in the first instance, but also electricity, and water-power. The conditions under which these sources of power are developed vary so widely from one place to another that no one of these industries could be effectively conducted under a single, uniform, centralized system; there must be the utmost elasticity and variety of method, such as can only be got from individual enterprise. Nevertheless such industries are concerned with the exploitation of vital and irreplaceable national assets, which must not be wastefully used. For that reason, and also because the harmonious working of these industries is more vital to the nation's well-being than that of any others (for a coal-strike stops everything else, a cotton-strike only stops cotton), it is necessary that the community should exercise a more direct influence over them than over other industries. What is needed is something intermediate between direct public control and unqualified private enterprise.

A means of finding such an intermediate method has been worked out in the case of the coal industry,[1] and it is capable of being applied also (*mutatis mutandis*) in the kindred industries of electric supply and water-power. It is that the State should acquire all mineral rights, and place the administration of them in the hands of a strongly constituted Statutory Commission, whose powers would be defined by Act of Parliament. The commission would grant leases of workable coal-seams, either to private companies or to public bodies; and it would use the leasing-power to bring the mines

[1] See "The Problem of the Mines," by A. D. MacNair, in "Essays in Liberalism."

together in suitable groups, to encourage various experiments in methods of production, and to require certain conditions as to safety, as to the general conditions of work, and as to the organization and control of labour. On the same principle a Statutory Commission might take charge of our inadequate supplies of water-power, increasing them by impounding reservoirs in barren valleys, and leasing the use of them to municipal corporations or power companies. In the Liberal State it is probable that some such method of systematically organizing and controlling the sources of power while leaving the actual working of them to various appropriate bodies, public and private, will be widely employed.

A society in which so many non-capitalistic forms of industrial organization are used for such important purposes cannot accurately be described as purely capitalistic: it will, in truth, be remarkable for the variety of its methods, and for the use of different modes of organization, each for its appropriate purpose; and in this it will shortly be distinguished from the rigid uniformity of the Socialist mode.

VIII. INDUSTRIAL SELF-GOVERNMENT

But there is a yet more important respect in which the industrial system in the Liberal State will depart from pure Capitalism. Even in those industries wherein the control of private entrepreneurs or company directors is most effective, they will not enjoy an unqualified control. Over the processes of manufacture, indeed,—over the organization of the factory, and over the methods of marketing,—their control will be complete, for these are highly expert functions, which cannot be competently performed by committees chosen by ballot. But there are other aspects of the complex industrial process in regard to which the claim of the directing class to supremacy stands on quite a different footing. The principles upon which the wealth produced by co-operative effort should be distributed among the co-operating factors—the rates of wages and the hours and conditions of labour—the influence of factory organization upon the minds and bodies of the work-people—in short, all the human aspects of the industrial order—present problems upon which neither management nor capital can have any right to exercise dictatorial powers ; and for all these matters, which especially affect the freedom and security of the worker, the Liberal State will have brought into being a wholesome system of industrial self-government, wherein each of the contributory factors will have its appropriate share.

Even to-day there is a system of divided control in these matters. The State has asserted its power of insisting upon certain conditions of decency through Factory Acts, Employers' Liability Acts, and in other ways ; and its inspectors exercise in these respects a real share of control over the industrial process. The trade unions have made good their claim to be consulted upon all questions affecting wages and the hours and conditions of labour ; nay, they have gone further, and established a whole body of trade usages, often of a kind that gravely hampers production, which no employer dare disregard. Even to-day, therefore, the power of capital and management is very far indeed from being dictatorial. But the interventions of the State, though they have been beneficent, are apt to be somewhat inelastic, and are often too generalized to fit the varying conditions of different industries. On the other hand, the power of the trade unions as representing the body of workmen is a power wielded in conflict, not in co-operation; and the relations between them and the employers' bodies are too often confused on both sides by ignorance of relevant facts, and poisoned by mutual suspicion. Not until divided control wielded in incessant hostility is replaced by co-operative control exercised through open discussions based upon full knowledge, will the co-ordinated effort of all the factors in production, which is essential for national well-being, be effectively realized.

It will be realized in the Liberal State by the establishment of an efficient system of industrial self-government at several different stages. There will be shop committees in individual factories, including spokesmen of the management and of various types of workers, and charged with the duty of ensuring that the system works smoothly and humanely, that injustices and hardships are avoided, and that the necessary discipline of the factory is not tyrannically enforced. But as the organization and functions of these bodies must vary widely from one industry to another, and even from one factory to another, they cannot be set up by any Act of Parliament. In so far as they are established by a superior authority, it will be, and can only be, by an authority which can speak for an industry as a whole.

Yet more important, there will be in every industry regular and organized methods for the co-operative determination of the conditions which are to hold good in the industry as a whole. On each of these Boards or Councils there will be equal representation of the directorate and of the work-people, the latter represented by their skilled trade union officials; and there may also be, as in the Trade Boards of to-day, an external and impartial element. It will be the function of these bodies to fix, and to revise from time to time, the standard wage rates for each grade of labour, the hours and conditions of work, the rules as to overtime, and so forth; and the decisions at which they arrive will be legally binding upon all firms engaged in the industry.

But this vitally important work cannot be satisfactorily done unless those who take part in it have full and adequate knowledge of the conditions existing in the industry, its prospects, and the extent to which it is able to bear the burden imposed upon it. Without such knowledge friction and misunderstanding are inevitable. Therefore it will be provided by law that in every industry there must be a return at regular intervals which will show (for the industry as a whole) how production and sales have risen and fallen, what is the cost of materials, how much of the gross product is being expended in wages, in salaries, in general overhead charges, in interest on capital. With such knowledge before them, these responsible bodies will be able to fix standard wage rates in such a way as to satisfy all who are concerned.

But the "standard wage," thus fixed will not form the whole of the worker's share in the product of the industry to which his strength is given. It will form only one (though the largest) of three elements in what Lord Cowdray has aptly described as the "ideal wage." The other elements will be (1) payment for additional effort put forth, beyond the average, either by the individual worker or (where this is not traceable) by a group of workers; and (2) some share in any special prosperity enjoyed by the firm in which the worker is employed, since this prosperity, though it may be mainly due to the enterprise of the direction, will always be in part due to the energy and goodwill of the workers. It is essential that these variable elements in the worker's remuneration should not be dependent upon the beneficence of his employer, but should come to him as by right, in accordance with fixed principles, the application of which he can understand and check. But it is obvious that no uniform general law can be laid down either for payment by results or for profit-sharing of the kind described. The conditions of work vary so widely from industry to industry, and even in different parts of the same industry, that no universal practice could be dictated, or would work fairly if it were imposed. But it would be practicable for the principles of these forms of payment to be worked out for each industry by the representative bodies which deal with wages, hours, and conditions. This method of decision would enable the worker to feel that he was being paid on a just basis; and the suspicion that systems of profit-sharing are only tricks to cozen the worker would be dispelled. By such means as these, under a system of industrial self-government, it will be ensured that the industry yields to the workers as large a share of its product as it can afford; the workers will be stimulated to put forth their maximum effort; and they will be supplied, over and above their "living wage," with a variable margin which will be available for saving.

Yet more important than all this will be the task of guarding against insecurity which is not due to the worker's fault; against unemployment, against disability due to sickness or accident, against an unprovided old age. In recent years the State has tried to deal with the task of combating these sources of insecurity, which are the most fundamental evils of the existing order. It has created a system of unemployment insurance, a system of insurance against sickness, and a system of old age pensions. But the State can only deal with the problem in a very generalized way, granting a flat rate of benefit or of pension, and making no allowance for different wage rates and the varying standards of living which they represent. Partly for this reason, it has been often urged that the function of insurance should be wholly transferred from the State to individual industries. But this is an impracticable and undesirable proposal, as we shall see when in a later chapter we come to deal with the immediate practical problem as it faces us to-day.[1] The State must continue to perform this function for industry as a whole, but what it does will have to be supplemented by each industry for itself, by means of levies on every firm in proportion to the number of its employees, on a basis agreed upon by both sides in the councils of the industry. In this way unemployment will first be dealt with, a fund being built up during periods of good trade which will ensure that the reserves of the industrial army, thrown out of work during periods of bad trade, will receive a decent maintenance proportionate to their normal scale of living. And in the same manner pensions will also be provided, so that when the time comes for retirement the workman, like the teacher or the civil servant, will have, as by right, an assured retiring allowance for the term of his life to enable him to live in self-respect. This system will be in full working order in the ideal Liberal State. It will be controlled and directed, in the main, by the co-operative factors of industry, and the cost of it will be borne by industry. Thus all who contribute to the creation of the nation's wealth will feel that they are treated as citizens and as men, not as mere tools to be thrown aside when they have served their turn. Nothing will contribute more than this national provision against avoidable insecurity to stimulate

[1] See Chap. IV, p. 160.

men to do their honest best, and to earn all that they can during their years of strength. Nothing, moreover, will form a greater inducement to saving and thrift ; for it will be worth a man's while to increase the provision for his old age, or to make provision for his children, when he knows that he will have a secure basis to build upon.

The burden will fall upon industry, as it is right that it should. But it may be objected that the burden will be too heavy for industry to bear, and that it will be crippled. Those who are tempted to make this objection forget that the whole system will be fixed in consultation by the factors concerned, and will be based upon clear and adequate knowledge of the facts : it will be in view of the actual productive power of the industry that all the rates will be fixed and varied—wage rates, systems of profit sharing, unemployment and pension contributions. Frank disclosure of the facts, and consultation thereupon, will be the foundation of everything. And one of the essential facts which cannot be overlooked will be the necessity of giving a fair remuneration to capital if it is to be attracted to the industry. The more widely the practice of saving and investment grows, the more clearly this will be realized.

The objection that the burden will be too heavy for industry to bear also overlooks another set of facts, not less important. It is that industry must in any case bear the burden of unemployment pay, and of unprovided old age. It bears it to-day, in the form of rates and taxes. And, since the work is to-day imperfectly and cruelly done (though at great cost), industry also has to bear the further and immeasurable burden of supporting a great mass of preventible weakness and inefficiency—of paying for the upkeep of under-nourished children and anæmic mothers, and for the cost of dealing with the crime that often results from the drunkenness of despair. Nor is this all: industry has to bear the burden of working with discontented and demoralized work-people, many of whom have convinced themselves that they are justified in deliberately and systematically doing less than their best; and this is a burden too great to be calculated. But even this is not the end. Under the conditions of to-day periods of bad trade are exaggerated by the fact that the spending power of masses of people is suddenly reduced. A system such as we have described, which would transfer some of the surplus profits of "boom" years to pay for the adequate maintenance of unemployed men during "slump" years, would tend to equalize demand in the main articles of consumption, and would thus be beneficial to industry.

Such will be the results, in the Liberal State, of a rational system of industrial self-government, applied to the regulation not of the expert functions of management, but to the human side of industry to which it is appropriate.

It is important to keep in mind this distinction between the expert side and the human side of industry; for it is essential to sound thinking on these questions. Not in this sphere alone, but throughout the whole range of human activities, there are some things that can be satisfactorily decided by discussion and voting, and others that definitely cannot. The medical profession, as a whole, for example, might very well define certain general rules which should govern the action of all members of the profession in their relations with one another and with their patients; but if they tried, by ballot vote, to decide upon the treatment which should be adopted by specialists in heart disease, the results must be ruinous. The things that can be decided "democratically" by a vote are the things that affect the justice or fairness of human relationships; the things that cannot be so decided are the things that depend upon individual genius and expert knowledge. In the industrial process it is seldom difficult to see where this line should be drawn. "Democratic control" can be applied with advantage to the regulation of the industrial process in so far as it affects the mutual relationships of those who take part in the process. It cannot, without ruinous consequences, be applied to those aspects of the work which depend upon individual capacity and knowledge. The fundamental defect of most Socialist schemes of "democratic control" is that they slur over this vital distinction, and insist upon settling both kinds of questions by discussion and voting. The fundamental defect of most Conservative opposition to schemes of reform is that it refuses to recognize that there *is* a sphere in industry to which discussion and voting are appropriate.

IX. A NATIONAL INDUSTRIAL COUNCIL

We have drawn the outlines of a system of self-government in particular industries which would afford a means of dealing with the problems that lie at the roots of industrial efficiency, and of providing the material foundations of liberty. This system, though it would be an immense advance upon the conditions of to-day, would nevertheless easily and naturally arise out of them: it would be an orderly development and co-ordination of the functions now performed by trade unions and employers' federations, the main difference being that while to-day these functions are carried on in conflict and in an atmosphere of suspicion, under the system we have described they would be carried on in co-operation and with adequate knowledge of the facts.

But the system as we have described it still lacks its keystone. The keystone will be a National Industrial Council, established by Act of Parliament, and including representatives of management and of labour in all the principal industries. This National Council will not merely be the apex of the structure of industrial self-government, it will be in some degree its foundation, and it will have to be established before the system as a whole can be brought into working order. For although Trade Boards already exist in some industries and Joint Industrial Councils in others, giving some foreshadowing of the future system, there are a number of industries, including some of the most important, in which no such mode of organization has yet been found practicable. The difficulty has arisen from the fact that industries are so interwoven with one another that it is hard to draw rigid lines between them. One firm will carry on work that might be classified under several different industries ; one trade union will have members engaged in a number of industries ; one industry will be concerned with a number of trade unions. For these reasons the more complex industries cannot easily organize themselves ; and any attempt to draw hard-and-fast lines by parliamentary enactment would be doomed to failure. The only solution of the difficulty is that of calling upon industry as a whole to organize itself, and supplying it with the means of doing so ; and the means will be the National Industrial Council. Where clear lines of division between industries already exist, it will recognize them ; where they can be usefully drawn, it will draw them ; and in some cases of exceptional complexity it will adopt the device of creating special committees to perform the functions elsewhere entrusted to Joint Councils of the normal pattern.

Another kindred function will also naturally fall to the National Council. The close interrelation which makes a delimitation of industries difficult also makes it impossible for them to conduct their affairs as if they were in water-tight compartments. A decision arrived at in one industry regarding hours of work or factory organization or unemployment benefit may deeply influence a neighbouring industry; and for this reason some means of co-ordination, some mode of common discussion of these points of overlapping, must be essential. It would be provided by the National Industrial Council.

But these functions of definition and co-ordination, important as they will be—and they will be essential to the efficient working of any system of self-government by industries—will not by any means exhaust the functions of the National Industrial Council. The creation of this body will mean that those who are most directly concerned are called into counsel for the determination of the nation's industrial policy; and once the Council is established, it will inevitably be called upon to express its judgment upon all questions that directly affect the nation's industrial life. It cannot be given the final determining voice; for that must be reserved to Parliament, which speaks for the community as a whole, and not merely for the active factors in production. But it is clear that no government or parliament could afford to disregard or brush aside any clear expression of opinion by a body so many-sided, and so obviously competent. Formally and technically the National Industrial Council must be only an advisory body on legislative questions, and, therefore, it cannot be accurately described (in the loose phrase which is often employed) as an "industrial parliament." But in practice it will become the main arena of discussion on all questions of purely industrial policy, and every industrial measure will be referred to its judgment before being enacted by Parliament. Indeed, it may very well be given more direct powers than this: it ought to have the right of initiating legislative proposals on industrial questions, which would be laid as by right before Parliament, and would in some cases be passed very rapidly into law, perhaps after merely lying on the table in both Houses for a defined time, in order to give opportunity for the raising of debate on any questionable point. Such a mode of procedure, without impairing the sovereign power and the ultimate responsibility of Parliament, would in fact, though not in theory, amount to a substantial delegation of the power now wielded by Parliament—or rather, by the Cabinet and the government departments acting under the cloak of Parliament. It would be a mode of devolution, which may be described as "functional devolution," and it would be a very real enlargement and refinement of self-government.

It is, indeed, difficult to exaggerate the value of such a system, whether as a means of relieving the preposterous burden which is rapidly reducing Parliament to impotence, or as a means of facilitating industrial reforms along lines that would be elastic, and adaptable to the varied conditions of different industries. During the last century the community has undertaken, on a steadily increasing scale, the duty of regulating industry, as a means of securing justice and liberty. This function has necessarily fallen upon Parliament, because it was the only body which could speak and act for the whole community.

But Parliament is not conspicuously well-organized for such work, seeing that it is only by accident that its membership includes men who can speak with knowledge of the conditions existing in particular industries; nor, loaded as it is with other duties, can it devote much time or systematic attention to these subjects. And from these conditions certain unfortunate results have arisen. In the first place, the work of industrial regulation has not been notably well done: in such a matter as railway legislation, for example, too little attention has often been paid to the needs of the trading community and of the fare-paying public. In the second place, the overloading of Parliament has led to a growth of what is called "bureaucracy," that is, the exercise of unchecked or insufficiently checked authority by permanent officials, and this has been specially notable in regard to industry. In the third place, the fact that Parliament was the only field for the discussion of industrial problems has led to a perturbing growth of what may be called representation by interests, which has largely distorted the character of the representative system.

All these dangerous developments would be checked by the working of a National Industrial Council, and they would be checked without any invasion of the ultimate sovereign authority of Parliament. The legislative regulation of industry would be based upon far deeper and more many-sided knowledge and discussion. Bureaucracy would find itself exposed to a much more competent and healthy criticism. The interests (whether trade unions or employers' associations) which are now scrambling for seats in Parliament would find that they had, and that they all equally had, direct and easy access to the body in which the most practical discussions took place. And Parliament would be relieved of a great mass of work which now distracts it from its primary purpose of criticizing the Government, and exercising a watchful control over national policy as a whole.

Thus the creation of a healthy system of industrial self-government may be expected not only to restore peace in industry by establishing justice and the conditions necessary to free enterprise; it will also help to strengthen and revivify the national system of government.

X. RELIGION—THE PRESS—SCIENCE AND THE ARTS LOCAL GOVERNMENT

The picture which we have attempted to draw of the structure and working of the future Liberal State is very far indeed from being complete. We have, for example, said nothing about religion, or about the attitude which the Liberal State will adopt towards the churches. This is not because any Liberal undervalues the powerful influence of religion upon the life of society: in the Liberal State, as at every stage of human progress, religious teaching will provide the highest stimulus towards that spirit of altruism without which no community can thrive. But just for this reason Liberalism has always held that religion is, of all aspects of life, the one which stands most in need of unfettered freedom: it holds in abomination the attempts which States have often made to enslave the minds of their subjects by getting control over the Churches. The Liberal State, therefore, will not meddle in any degree with the religious beliefs or observances of its citizens, so long as these do not endanger the health or the morals of the community; it will be very chary of interference even on these grounds; it will leave to every church or group of believers the fullest powers of self-government; and religious differences will cease to be the cause of political controversies.

Again, we have said nothing about the Press, which has become so powerful a factor in the life of every civilized community that it has earned for itself the designation of the "Fourth Estate." To secure complete freedom for the Press has always been one of the fundamental aims of Liberalism; and in a sense this aim has been attained, since there is no body of opinion, however unpopular, which is not free to obtain such publicity as it can organize, so long as it does not challenge public law and order. But we are still far from having secured the highest freedom for the Press—freedom from the dictation of wealth, from corrupting influences, and from the temptation to employ its immense power for the deception rather than the enlightenment of the community. This is one of the greatest problems of the future for democracy; and perhaps it will only be solved by the education of democracy. Assuredly it will not be solved by the device of Socialism—by nationalizing the whole business of writing, printing, and publishing. Conceive the position, in the Socialist State, of a small body of advocates of an unpopular idea—and all great ideas begin by being unpopular. They would have no capital of their own wherewith to finance books, pamphlets, and newspapers, nor would they be able to borrow it. They would have to trust to the tender mercies of a government department controlled by a party chief, or to a guild of printers who might refuse to disseminate ideas of which they disapproved. Is it not plain that a censorship even more merciless than that of Napoleon would be the inevitable result of such conditions? The ground given for refusing to publish unpopular ideas might be the cogent ground that they would not pay, and that public funds must not be wasted on them; but the plausibility of this explanation would not alter the fact that publication would be refused; and one of the foundation-stones of liberty would be destroyed. There is no better illustration of the danger which the Socialist project threatens to liberty, and therefore to progress, and of the vital importance of giving freedom to private enterprise. We saw during the war some of the evils of a government-regulated Press. We must have no more of them; and a free Press will be one of the essential features of the Liberal State.

Yet again, we have said nothing about the creative work of organized science and research, and the means of ensuring to it at once adequate support and full freedom: in an ever-increasing degree, our prosperity and well-being will depend in the future upon the wisdom with which we recognize and provide for this need. Nor have we touched upon letters, drama and the arts, or attempted to define the means by which they can be enabled to wield more fully their ennobling and refining influence upon the minds of men. They need, above all things, freedom rather than rigid organization; and they will do their work the more effectively in proportion as freedom is made more real for all men, and as it becomes possible for the citizen to be less engrossed in livelihood, and to give more of his thought to rational living. In these spheres, as in all others, the fundamental problem is the problem of reconciling communal support and encouragement with full freedom for individual inspiration—the problem of so using the power of the community that it shall not restrain liberty, but make it more real. The habit of mind which regards liberty as the end to be aimed at, and is perpetually watchful and suspicious of any attempt to replace it by even the most efficient organization ; the habit of mind which is willing to use communal power only so far as it enlarges liberty—this is the Liberal habit of mind, and it is the only safe guide in dealing with those high activities whose very breath of life is freedom.

We can do no more than mention these vitally important aspects of a healthy society, and pass on ; because the scope and design of this little book confine us to the discussion of those questions of civic and economic organization with which politics are primarily concerned. Even within this restricted field, there are great and important subjects upon which we can only touch lightly, not because they are of less importance than the problems of industrial organization to which we have given so much space, but because they are in a sense less novel, less urgent, and less subject to vehement party controversy.

Thus we have only referred in passing to the immense subject of local government. Our existing system of local government has in all its main features been created by Liberalism ; and the fact that with us local authorities enjoy a far higher degree of autonomy than is usual in European countries is due to the Liberal belief that questions of common interest should so far as possible be determined by those who are most directly concerned. But it is plain that, for the expansion of freedom and self-government, a still further development of the system is required ; and the working out of this development is one of the tasks to which Liberalism looks forward.

This raises many questions of high importance, which cannot be fully discussed here. What is the proper sphere of local government ? Can it be much extended beyond the fields of public order, health, and education, to which it is now in the main confined? What should be the relation between local authorities and private enterprise, not merely in the commercial sphere, but in education and in charitable work? Should the local authority be in the main confined to regulation in all fields in which private enterprise can efficiently operate? Should it undertake public services of a monopolistic type, and if so, should it be enabled to destroy or forbid competition, for example in transport? Should it be encouraged to attempt other work in which it will compete directly with private enterprise? How can local self-government be made more real in the smaller areas, and particularly in villages? How can the existing larger authorities be co-ordinated or federated, so as to make joint action possible in many directions in which it is desirable? Can this be combined with a system of devolution which would relieve Parliament from some part of the pressure of work that makes it inefficient? How can the distribution of local burdens be adjusted so as to be fair both to the citizens of a given area, and also as between rich and poor areas? What should be the relations between local authorities and the central government, and how shall we steer between the Scylla of local anarchy and the Charybdis of bureaucratic domination?

These are questions of vital importance, but we cannot discuss them here. It must suffice to lay down, both dogmatically and vaguely, how some of these problems will be solved in the ideal Liberal State. Self-government will be more real and active than it is to-day in the smallest units, such as the village or parish, where the citizen is in daily contact with the work of his representatives. At every stage there will be an increased unity of control, which will get rid of such causes of overlapping as are now presented by the co-existence of municipalities and boards of guardians; and in every defined area there will be one central authority responsible for regulating the whole of the communal work within its sphere and for determining how much shall be spent on each department of this work. But it will be held to be the function of these authorities to ensure that the labours of public service are efficiently performed, rather than to engross them in its own hands; and for this purpose they will enlist from every quarter all useful co-operation. One of the ways in which this will be done will be an enlargement of the existing practice of adding to various committees co-opted members possessed of special gifts or knowledge, who will thus be enabled to render useful service without invading the ultimate financial authority of the ruling body: this device is one of the most profitable of recent inventions in government, because, while preserving the supremacy of the elected body, it saves much valuable ability, eager for public service, from being wasted.

The cost of local administration in the Liberal State will be divided, as now, between the central government and the local authority; the central government will bear a larger share of the cost of some services than it does to-day; but in all cases the share borne by the local authority will be sufficiently large to bring home to the ratepayers and their representatives the importance of careful economy. The central contribution will be determined partly by the amount of work to be done (e.g. the number of children to be educated or of poor persons to be maintained), and partly by the efficiency of the service rendered, in order to combine central supervision with local responsibility. The local contribution will be raised, on a revised rating system, in such a way as to exact a direct payment proportionate to his means from every resident not in receipt of relief; but a substantial part of the burden will be levied upon the site-value of land, rather than upon the value of the buildings erected on it, in order to encourage, instead of penalizing, enterprise in making improvements

Finally, there will be a series of co-ordinating bodies for large regions, which will be elected by the constituent authorities, in order to avoid a multiplication of elections, which (as American experience shows) is apt to weaken the sense of responsibility, and to diminish the real power of the elector by bewildering him. These bodies will have a triple function to perform. In certain fields (such as communications, water supply, or education) they will make possible a more systematic treatment of the problems than is now possible. They will bring about an equalization of burdens as between rich and poor areas in those services, such as poor relief, which press with undue weight upon the poorer areas; though it should not be forgotten that the burden of poor relief will have been immensely lightened when the system of dealing with unemployment and pensions already described has been brought into operation. And, finally, these great regional authorities will undertake much of the work now performed by Parliament or by government departments, notably legislation for the conferment (within defined limits) of powers upon local bodies, the revision of administrative areas, and much of the work of criticizing and stimulating the administration of local authorities. This will result on the one hand in a real relief of Parliament, and on the other in a real qualification of the growing power of bureaucracy. And the system as a whole will have the effect of making self-government more real for each group in the matters that directly affect it, and of bringing home more directly to every citizen his share of responsibility for the common welfare.

XI. LIBERAL PRINCIPLES IN TAXATION

We have left to the last one of the most fundamental of political problems, a problem the right solution of which lies at the root of all progress in freedom and self-government, as their whole history demonstrates—the problem of national finance and of the right distribution of national burdens. It is impossible here to enter upon any serious discussion of the vast and intricate questions which are involved in this theme. In particular, we shall not attempt to deal with the terrible and urgent difficulties left by the war. These are problems of the actual, not of the ideal, and we shall have something to say about them in that connexion when we come to deal with the immediate tasks of Liberalism.

Here we must be content to lay down certain broad principles which British Liberalism has wrought out during the last hundred years. They have involved a profound revolution in the national economy. They have been terribly tested by the ordeal of the Great War, and have triumphantly survived the test. Whatever changes may be made in the economic structure of the nation, these principles will continue to guide the statesmanship of the ideal Liberal State.

All taxation is confiscation. It is the confiscation for communal purposes, by the power of the State, of part of the wealth possessed by individuals. This fact renders absurd and meaningless the complaint often made, especially by Conservatives, that this or that tax is "confiscatory." Since every tax, whether direct or indirect, confiscates part of the individual citizen's wealth, the only question for statesmanship is the question, What forms of confiscation will be least harmful? But this plain fact is equally fatal to the illusion which seems to be cherished by the Labour party that taxation is a good thing in itself. It is a bad thing in itself (though necessary), in so far as it deprives a man of what he has legitimately earned by his own efforts, and to that extent robs him of the means of displaying enterprise and of making the most of his own gifts, and the best of his own life, in his own way. It transfers this power from the free man to the State—and the State always means, in practice, a limited number of fallible men.

Hence the first Liberal principle in taxation is that the State should not take from the individual citizen one penny more than is necessary for the efficient service of those common interests which can only be met by communal action. These common interests are large, and will grow larger; the cost of serving them is great, and will grow greater. All the more reason why the utmost care should be taken that not a penny of the money raised to serve them is wasted, and why every claim for public funds for any purpose which is not necessary for the nation's well-being should be very strictly scrutinized—especially claims for military purposes beyond what is absolutely essential for security. It is because this principle is of the very marrow of Liberalism that, during the period of reckless extravagance which followed the Great War, the voice of the small group of free Liberals, and their voice alone, consistently demanded drastic reductions of all expenditures save those on essential national services, such as education.

The second principle is that, as an essential means of bringing home to every citizen a sense of responsibility for the policy and action of the State, every man or woman whose income is above the subsistence level should be required to make some definite and conscious contribution, however small, to the common burdens. In a healthy, prosperous, and well-ordered State, such as the Liberal State will be if our national prosperity revives, there should be very few below the subsistence level. The contribution demanded from those who are near the subsistence level ought of course to be very small, but it ought to be definite ; otherwise democracy will be apt to connote irresponsibility. Any man who can meet his trade union levy, or pay for his regular glass of beer, can afford to contribute some pittance towards the upkeep of the State, which makes life itself possible for him. The financial programme of the Labour party (which proposes to impose almost the whole burden of national government upon those who have more than £500 a year) flagrantly violates this principle. It would set up a privileged majority of 8,000,000 families who would determine the policy of the State, but would feel no financial responsibility for this policy, since the whole cost would be imposed upon a politically impotent minority of 2,000,000 families. This would destroy freedom for the minority, while, for the majority, it would viciously divorce freedom from its essential correlative, responsibility.

The third principle is that (subject to the proviso just laid down) taxation should be graduated according to the capacity of the citizen to bear the burden without loss of efficiency. This principle absolutely condemns the practice of raising the national revenue mainly by indirect taxes upon necessaries, which was pursued before the period of Liberal ascendancy, and is still largely pursued in protectionist States ; for taxes upon articles of general consumption fall with special severity upon the poor. The aim can best be attained by means of a graduated income-tax; and the ideal system would be one in which, while a merely nominal tax was levied upon those just above the subsistence level, the rate should be progressively increased until it reached a very high level on undesirably large incomes. Owing to the difficulty of levying income-tax on weekly wages, this ideal has never been realized, and the weekly wage-earner is practically taxed only on articles of consumption—with the unfortunate consequence that a poor widow with a large family may be called upon to pay (in the taxes on tea and sugar) more than a prosperous artisan. Nevertheless the principle of graduation has already been carried so far by Liberal statesmanship that income-tax ranges from 1*d.* in the pound on the lowest grade of income assessed to this tax, up to 11*s.* in the pound on the largest incomes. In the ideal Liberal State (when a reasonable security for the wage-earner has been attained, and the total income of the nation is more fairly distributed) income-tax will begin just above the subsistence level; and then —and not till then—indirect taxation (except, for social reasons, on certain luxuries) will be wholly abolished.

The fourth principle is that all the wealth taken by the instrument of taxation from the pockets of individual citizens should pass to the Treasury and be accounted for, and that none of it should be diverted into private pockets. This principle is violated by any system of protective duties. For if foreign boots (for example) are taxed, the price of all boots rises to a greater or less extent; and the extra price of the home-manufactured boots (which forms a tax upon all purchasers, and is most severely felt by the poorest) goes into the pockets of the home manufacturers. In many cases such a tax would extract from the public, for private advantage, ten or twenty times as much wealth as it would bring into the Treasury. And on this principle, which is one of the foundations of the economic doctrine of Free Trade, Liberalism finds itself in sharp conflict with the bulk of the Conservative party.

The fifth principle is that taxation which penalizes thrift, or which interferes with industry or bears with especial severity upon it, should so far as possible be avoided. Of course all taxation may be said to have these effects in some degree; but some taxes are worse than others. Thus the requirement that every cheque should be stamped penalizes thrift by deterring people from opening small accounts with a bank; and nothing does more to encourage thrift than the possession of a bank account. Thus, again, the Excess Profits Duty, which may have been defensible as a war measure, had very deleterious effects after the war, because it discouraged enterprise in many cases, and encouraged reckless speculation in others; whilst it was peculiarly open to various forms of dishonest evasion, and so lowered the standard of commercial morality. Even a very high income-tax may have unhappy effects of this kind; for the man who knows that, while he must bear all his own losses, the bulk of any profits he may make will be taken from him, is not encouraged to undertake risky ventures which might be very desirable in the public interest. This is why the proposal of the Labour party to impose practically the whole burden of taxation upon incomes of more than £500 would defeat its own purpose. It would, indeed, forcibly redistribute wealth; but it would also put a stop to the initiative which makes the creation of wealth possible. The very necessary task of bringing about a juster distribution of the national income must, in the main, be achieved by other means than those of the tax-gatherer, and at an earlier stage. It must be achieved by industrial reorganization, not by financial devices.

The sixth principle is that in normal times the direct taxation of capital is highly inexpedient, because it creates a sense of insecurity which deters saving; but this does not imply that such a device, even on a heroic scale, might not be practicable at a moment of national crisis when the people were stirred to a high pitch of readiness for sacrifice. There is, however, one great and important exception to this principle. Large accumulations of capital may legitimately be heavily taxed at the death of the accumulator, because he will have enjoyed the fullest opportunity of making use of the wealth he has earned. To take a large proportion of a dead man's fortune (provided that enough is left to make ample provision for his children) will not discourage enterprise on the part either of the dead man or of his heirs, nor will it seriously weaken the motives to thrift; but it forms a legitimate mode of redistributing wealth. Hence the Death Duties (which were a Liberal invention) have become an essential element in the British system of taxation; and they are capable of expansion.

The seventh principle is that any form of taxation which can be made to serve a socially desirable purpose is to be preferred on that ground. Into this category fall taxes upon any luxuries which do not increase the well-being of the community, such as spirits and tobacco, or which are used mainly for purposes of ostentation; but no such tax should be imposed in such a way as to involve protection, and thus to take from the community more than is received by the Treasury. To this category may also be referred a system of taxation on land which would debar men from withholding from use land which is needed for any useful purpose; for such a system would encourage enterprise by making it the interest of every landowner to see that his land was put to the most profitable use. In the Liberal State such taxes will be freely employed. But they will not form a large element in the national revenue, which will depend mainly upon the direct and honest method of the income-tax.

XII. CONCLUSION

The description which we have attempted to give of the structure and working of the Liberal State is, it may be feared, somewhat bald and abstract; it deals with principles and theories more than with those vivid descriptions of mechanical marvels and of perfected human beings with which the Socialist Utopia-monger loves to indulge his fancy. Such as it is, it will not, in all its details, commend itself to every Liberal. Indeed, no such description would do this; for it is of the essence of Liberalism that it encourages variety of opinion among those who share a common faith in liberty as the mainspring of human progress. It is not intended as a detailed programme of action, or as a scheme capable of being promptly embodied in legislation in all its parts; for it covers many subjects upon which a vast deal of study and inquiry is still needed. Nor is it meant as the description of an ultimate Utopia for humanity: that is a vision which no Liberal would have the insolence to define, since the essence of his creed is a belief in the unpredictable capacity of the human mind and will. It is designed to give a more or less concrete embodiment to an ideal which is not easily grasped when it is expressed only in general terms: the ideal of using the power and the goodwill of the community, not for the purpose of manufacturing a sterile, uniform, and enforced material comfort, but for the purpose of creating such conditions as will make individual liberty progressively more real and more fruitful; the ideal of an enlarging freedom, resting on and protected by law, as the best hope of progress and happiness for men.

But (some reader may ask) are you justified in giving the name of Liberalism to the aims you have set forth? Are these not a new invention, out of accord with the past records of the Liberal party? Do they not constitute a departure from the policy of *laissez-faire* with which we have been taught to identify Liberalism?

If it were true that the kind of ideal we have tried to sketch was in disaccord with the traditions and the record of the Liberal party, the criticism would have some force, though it would not be decisive. But it is not true. And the answer to these questions is to be found in an analysis of the past achievements of Liberalism, to which we shall proceed in the next chapter of this book. For such an analysis will show that, in spite of all the differences of view which have from time to time emerged among Liberals, it is in fact towards some such ideal as we have sketched that Liberalism has steadily moved during the century of its existence as an organized force in British politics. And not only so, but when we look back to the conditions that existed a century ago when Liberalism began its work, the progress which has been made in every aspect of the policy we have here outlined will be found to have been infinitely greater than is usually recognized.

This chapter is mainly devoted to theories rather than to concrete details, which will be discussed in Chapter IV. For further reading see Hobhouse, "Liberalism" (Home University Library); Masterman, "The New Liberalism" (Parsons); Ramsay Muir, "Liberalism and Industry" (Constable); "Essays in Liberalism" (Collins); and, among older books, T. H. Green's "Principles of Political Obligation" and J. S. Mill's "Liberty," "Representative Government," and "Political Economy" (Bk. V.).

CHAPTER III

THE PAST ACHIEVEMENTS OF LIBERALISM

I. THE LIBERAL ACHIEVEMENT

THE history of British Liberalism may be said to begin with the general election which followed the Reform Act of 1832. Till then the Whigs, a group of great aristocrats, had been the party of progress. But whilst the Whigs believed in, and fought for, "civil and religious liberty," they held that it was most secure under the guardianship of an aristocracy. Anything but democrats, they upheld the power of Parliament against the Crown, but were unwilling to make Parliament a democratic body; they were advocates of toleration, but not of religious equality; they regarded established law as the main safeguard of liberty, but, precisely for that reason, were reluctant to contemplate any radical reconstruction of the social order, and of the system of law and custom on which it rested.

But after the Reform Act of 1832 Whig ministries found themselves supported by and dependent upon a mixed host of reformers, who had made up their minds to be content with nothing less than a complete reconstruction of the political and social order. There were philosophic Radicals of the school of Bentham, scientific economists who accepted the doctrines of Adam Smith and Ricardo, dissenters who had long suffered from various disabilities, members of the new class of capitalist manufacturers who were transforming British industry with their machines and factories, humanitarians who burned with indignation at the spectacle of human wretchedness and human cruelty, colonial enthusiasts who had conceived new ideals as to the right relationship between the mother-country and her colonies. The various elements in this diversified host differed widely among themselves, and from that day to this the Liberal party, which they brought into being, has included many different groups and schools of thought. But all were agreed as to the necessity of a far-reaching reconstruction; and all were united in the conviction that the aim of this reconstruction must be to make liberty more real for all citizens. By their combined if sometimes discordant efforts they carried out a series of great changes which transformed the condition of the British people.

No one who has any knowledge of the condition of things before 1830 will hesitate to admit that a great transformation was needed. Europe was under the domination of a group of reactionary despots who were bent upon suppressing every movement towards national unity or political liberty. The British colonies were either stagnant, or full of discontent, or both. In the homeland the mass of the people were suffering from such distresses as Britain had never known in the course of modern history; a reactionary government was tempted to take every cry of suffering as a threat of revolution; and many thoughtful observers believed that a violent and terrible upheaval was imminent. The country was loaded with a burden of debt left by the Napoleonic War, and the charges which it involved, being mainly met by taxes on necessaries, fell with especial weight upon the poor. The Industrial Revolution had turned upside down the old and settled social order which had made Britain, on the whole, a happy and prosperous country in the eighteenth century; and while the capitalist owners of the new factories were making great fortunes very rapidly, the mass of their workpeople had to labour for incredibly long hours, under very unhealthy conditions, to earn wages which were in many cases too scanty even for bare subsistence, though the standards of the time were terribly low. Little children of eight and even five years old were forced to work, sometimes for fourteen or fifteen hours a day; yet even with this pitiful aid, family incomes were so low that about one in four of the population were often in receipt of poor relief, and under the system then in vogue the acceptance of poor relief exposed its recipients to something very like slavery to the poor law authorities. Thanks in part to the disorganization of Europe, but still more to an unhealthy fiscal system, trade could not expand fast enough to keep pace with the growth of population and the development of the new machines. Unemployment was rife, and there was no means of providing for it except the Poor Law; for trade unions were only struggling into being, and were regarded with profound distrust. The new towns which had sprung into existence to house the new industrial population had no efficient system of government, and were incredibly ugly, dirty, cramped, and insanitary; moreover, they were devoid of all the apparatus of a decent civilization, lacking in most cases even an adequate supply of water; and two-thirds of the population were wholly illiterate. It may be doubted whether any country in Europe could show an uglier mass of misery than Britain displayed in those dark days, though she was the richest country in the world. It is no wonder that there was a constant menace of violent revolution, and that wild, crude, and contradictory schemes of social reorganization found ready hearers among the industrial population. All the fantastic theories, catchwords, and panaceas of the Socialist and the Syndicalist were in truth foreshadowed during these years.

What made things seem more hopeless was that the people did not possess the constitutional means of trying to remedy their own ills. For self-government had become a very unreal and meaningless thing in Britain, the land of its origin. All political power was in the hands of a small oligarchy of land-owners, who controlled both Houses of Parliament and almost the whole machinery of local government. The members of this oligarchy were mostly honourable, proud, and patriotic men. They had once been the natural leaders of the nation, in the not distant days when the greater part of the English people consisted of prosperous yeomen and peasants. But the great industrial revolution had ended that. Out of touch with the needs and feelings of the country, the ruling class lived in dread of revolution, and mistook every cry of anguish for a threat. The laws of the land were incredibly brutal and cruel: they imposed the penalty of death for over two hundred offences. Yet instead of doing anything of serious importance to amend the condition of the people, their rulers had, until within ten years of 1832, kept on adding new ferocities to this hideous code, with the idea that firm repressive action was the only way of avoiding an upheaval.

With a crude revolutionary movement, born of desperation, afoot on the one hand, and with a dangerous reactionary temper in control on the other, it seems little less than a miracle, to the serious student of that time, that a violent upheaval did not take place. Assuredly it would have taken place among any people less stolidly patient and moderate than the British people; and if it had come, it could have brought nothing but ruin, for it would have involved the collapse of the whole economic system by means of which, imperfect as it was, the people were enabled to obtain such sustenance as they got.

What was it that made it possible for Britain to escape from this desperate plight? Beyond any shadow of doubt it was the coming of Liberalism to power, and the remarkable work of reconstruction that Liberalism carried out. Within twenty years of 1832, though the social problem had by no means been solved, the worst evils had disappeared, and some measure of contentment and prosperity had returned to Britain and to the British Empire. The sovereign remedy by means of which this miracle of healing was achieved was the medicine of liberty, courageously and progressively applied. But the application of this remedy did not cease with the first period of reconstruction; for the evils to be dealt with were so vast and so complex that they took long to heal. The work went on steadily throughout the long period of Liberal ascendancy (1830–1874); it revived again whenever the Liberals obtained power; and it was never more active than during the eight years preceding the Great War of 1914. But even now, as we have seen, the task is far from being completed; and, as we have already tried to show, it is to a continued pursuit of the Liberal ideal of making freedom more real that we must still look for our extrication from the difficulties of to-day, which in many respects resemble those of a hundred years ago.

In the present chapter it is our purpose to show that during the ninety years which have passed since 1832 this ideal has been steadfastly pursued; and that great things have already been achieved under its inspiration. Labour orators (whose strong point is not historical knowledge) habitually tell their audiences that the Liberal party has done nothing for the working class: they trust, and for the most part safely trust, to the ignorance of their hearers. The more reputable and the better-informed leaders of the Labour party do not take this line; but they habitually assume that the task of Liberalism is accomplished, and that it was limited to political reform and never aimed at any real social amelioration. There is only one way of answering these false and shallow statements: by setting forth the irrefutable facts.

To do this in any full or adequate way would almost involve a narrative of the history of the nineteenth century. And as this is altogether beyond our scope in the present volume, we shall content ourselves with taking in turn the various aspects of the Liberal ideal in the order in which they were discussed in the last chapter, and showing how in each aspect—foreign policy, imperial policy, political reform, education and public health, industrial organization, and public finance—the work of our predecessors has led up to the work that still lies before us, and established the solid foundations upon which it is possible for us to build.

II. IN FOREIGN POLICY

Throughout the long period of Liberal ascendancy in British politics (1830–1874), when Europe was constantly disturbed by demands for political liberty or for national unity and independence, Britain was recognized as the steadiest friend of these causes;

and although she never went to war for them, her diplomatic influence, and still more the force of her example, had a great deal to do with the triumph of nationalist movements in various countries, and with the gradual adoption of the forms of parliamentary government in almost every European State. Liberal Britain was in truth regarded as the staunchest supporter of freedom. She played her part, and more than her part, in the organization of Europe into a group of free and self-governing nations, which was the necessary foundation of further progress.

Towards the close of this period, when Europe had begun to settle down after the Franco-Prussian war, a new period of international relations began: a period of watchful rivalry between groups of allied powers, who, following the example of Germany, began to arm themselves to the teeth. In this transformed world Britain had to consider what her attitude ought to be, and the Liberal point of view on these momentous issues was defined by Gladstone during the long debate on foreign politics which he carried on with Disraeli from 1878 to 1880. Gladstone laid down certain broad principles of foreign policy, which aroused a good deal of controversy at the time, but from which no sincere Liberal would to-day dissent.

The first principle is that the highest interest of this country is neither dominion nor prestige but peace. In saying this, Gladstone did not mean to advocate peace at any price, for he himself engaged in several necessary wars, and ran the risk of others. Nor did he mean that mere abstention from war on her own part would satisfy Britain's needs. He meant that what we need is nothing less than organized and settled peace throughout the world, without which trade and industry cannot thrive.

The second principle is that peace ought not to be

pursued by the false path of military alliances with one power or group of powers, even though the aim of such an alliance may honestly be to guard the peace against possible danger from another power or group of powers. There must be no "entangling alliances" such as that in which Britain had practically been involved with Turkey, and which had very nearly led to war with Russia in 1878. To this principle of avoiding entangling alliances British policy has ever since been faithful—with one real and one apparent exception. The real exception was the Anglo-Japanese alliance of 1902, which, having served its purpose of saving the Pacific from becoming the scene of European conflicts, has since been dissolved. The apparent exception was the understanding between France and Britain which became so close during the anxious years preceding the Great War. But this agreement was not an "entanglement" in Gladstone's sense. It did not pledge either party to military action; its sole aim was the removal of differences and the maintenance of peace by diplomatic co-operation; and it was so far from being exclusive that Sir Edward Grey strove to bring Germany into a similar understanding. In truth, the policy pursued by Britain in the years preceding the Great War was in full accord with the principles laid down by Gladstone.

For when Gladstone condemned "foreign entanglements" he did not mean that Britain ought to wash her hands of the troubles of Europe, and refuse to accept her share of responsibility for the common interests of civilization. On the contrary, he laid it down as his third principle that the true mode of pursuing general peace was in co-operation with other peoples, and by the employment of the Concert of Europe—then the only instrument, though an imperfect one, for the expression of the common will of civilization. In this respect, also, the principle as he defined it was loyally accepted by Liberal statesmen. As all Europe admitted, it was by the use of the Concert of Europe that Sir Edward Grey succeeded in averting the almost annual threats of war by which Europe was perturbed during the years 1906–1914; and he could have succeeded in averting the final menace of 1914 by the same means if Germany had only permitted the Concert of Europe to come into operation.

But, when all is said, the Concert of Europe (which meant the private diplomatic conferences of the Five Great Powers) was a very inadequate and imperfect means of pursuing peace. Gladstone recognized this when he laid it down as his fourth principle that in international relations all States should be treated as equals—not, of course, as equals in power, but as equals in the right to be consulted on matters of common moment. The old regime in foreign affairs offered no means of giving effective expression to this principle. Happily it has found an embodiment in the League of Nations. The League, indeed, provides an all but perfect exemplification of the Liberal ideal in international relations, since it combines organization for co-operative action with full recognition of the freedom of every member-State.

But Gladstone's ideal contemplated not only the equal treatment of all States already free, it contemplated also a steady expansion of freedom; and his fifth principle was that all the weight and influence which Britain could exercise in the councils of the nations should be used in favour of political freedom, and for the protection of oppressed peoples.

This being the proclaimed policy of Liberalism in the past, it is evident that the achievements of

Liberalism have prepared the way for, and are in complete accord with, that ideal system of international relations which we endeavoured to describe in the last chapter.

III. IN IMPERIAL POLICY

Even more completely has the Liberal policy of the past prepared the way for the ideal of a free British Commonwealth of partner nations; for this is a Liberal conception, and almost every step which has been taken towards its realization has been the work of Liberal statesmanship. It was, indeed, the Whig orator, Burke, who, on the occasion of the revolt of the American colonies (1775), gave the first clear expression to the inspiring idea that a group of free peoples might be bound together (as the self-governing members of the British Commonwealth are to-day bound), not by force or by any rigid economic ties, but by "ties light as air, yet strong as links of iron"—by pride in the same institutions of freedom, and by community of aims. But it was a little group of Liberal statesmen—Durham, Wakefield, Molesworth and Buller—who first set themselves, in the years following 1830, to translate this ideal into facts; and it was their work, and that of their successors, which fixed the character of the modern British Empire.

It is often said that Liberalism has always been indifferent to the Empire. And it is true that, especially in the middle of the nineteenth century, there were many Liberals, as there were also many Tories, who believed that the great colonies must in time become independent States, and desired to hasten this process; it is also true that Liberalism has always been out of sympathy with imperialism, if by that word is meant a spirit of domination which takes pride in the mere extension of dominion for its own sake. But it is also true that there have always been many Liberals who have desired and worked for the unity of the Empire; they have conceived of the empire, however, not as a mere dominion but as a brotherhood of free peoples, and have believed that the fellowship of freedom would prove to be a stronger bond of unity than any formal ties that could be invented.

Inspired by this ideal, they conferred complete self-government on Canada almost on the morrow of an open rebellion (1840); they turned Australia from a convict settlement despotically governed into a group of free States which were endowed with the fullest rights of autonomy (1855); they organized the colonization of New Zealand, and gave it self-governing powers within twelve years of the coming of the first settlers (1852); they conferred responsible government on Cape Colony (1871). It was but a continuance of this inspiring tradition when, in 1906–7, the full rights of self-government were conferred by a Liberal government upon the Transvaal and the Orange Free State, within five years of the close of a bitterly fought war. The magnanimity of this act astonished the world, but it was no more than the natural continuance of a traditional Liberal policy. The wisdom of this magnanimous policy of freedom has been very strikingly demonstrated by the course of events. Did not the wholehearted zeal and the glorious deeds of the Dominion troops in the Great War prove that the comradeship of freedom can yield a far stauncher loyalty than mere power and authority can ever inspire?

It is not only in the granting of self-government to the English-speaking colonies that Liberalism has played the chief part in defining the character of the modern British Empire, but quite as clearly in the treatment of backward peoples. Throughout the modern age, these peoples had been pitilessly exploited by all the white races in whose empires they were incorporated; and the iniquities of negro slavery were the worst sign of this exploitation. The very first legislative act of the first Liberal parliament, elected in 1832, was the emancipation of all the slaves in the British Empire, and the voting of a huge sum to buy their freedom from their masters. This struck the note of a new policy, which was largely inspired and deepened by the army of Christian missionaries whom Britain maintained. In every land where primitive peoples dwelt under the British flag it became one of the primary duties of the agents of British power to protect them against injustice, and to safeguard their rights and property. Nor was this all. When Britain adopted Free Trade she extended it to all the lands which she controlled; and this meant that there was access to these lands on equal terms for the traders of all nations. Thus, in these lands, Liberal policy had defined that it was the duty of the ruling State to act, not as if the territories existed solely for the advantage of the ruling race, but in the capacity of a trustee—a trustee for the subject peoples on the one hand, and for the civilized world on the other.

At the close of the Great War there was embodied, in the Covenant of the League of Nations, a sort of statement of the ideal principles upon which backward territories, administered by civilized governments, ought to be controlled. This statement appears in the mandatory clauses, which were intended to be applied only to the territories taken from Germany and Turkey. It represents the most progressive ideas of to-day in the sphere of colonial policy. And it is essentially based upon the actual practice which has been followed in the backward regions of the British Empire under the guidance of Liberal policy.

Plainly we are justified in claiming that in this sphere also Liberal policy in the past has been in key with the ideals we have conceived for the future. It has, in truth, made these ideals possible.

IV. IN THE ESTABLISHMENT OF POLITICAL DEMOCRACY

When we turn to the sphere of domestic reorganization, no one will deny to Liberalism the credit of having played the main part in shaping the machinery of democracy. The Reform Act of 1832, which began the history of the Liberal party, was followed by the Reform Act of 1867, which, though it was introduced by a Conservative government, was turned into a democratic measure by the Liberal opposition; and this in its turn was succeeded by the Act of 1884, which enfranchized the rural labourer and very nearly established manhood suffrage. But the enlargement of the franchise formed only a minor element in the establishment of democracy. Vote by ballot was needed to make it real, and this was a Liberal measure (1871). The restriction of the power of the House of Lords was a necessary supplement; and this was only achieved, after a fierce fight, in 1911. With these changes may be associated the opening of the civil service to brains rather than to influence, which was secured by the establishment of appointment by competitive examination in 1871. These measures gave to the nation as a whole, when its will was clearly formulated, the power of carrying it into effect.

Not less important, and in some ways even more directly beneficent, was the creation of a new system of local government. Elected Boards of Guardians replaced the old irresponsible Justices of the Peace in the management of the Poor Law; elected Municipal Councils gave for the first time to the towns a unified system of administration, and enabled them to begin the long fight against squalor and degradation: few greater services have been rendered to the British people than the creation of the system which made this work possible. Elected Boards of Health and other authorities, including, presently, School Boards, followed. These were all Liberal achievements. Later (1888) the counties were also equipped with representative councils. This Act, though it had been drafted by a Liberal statesman, was actually carried by a Conservative government. But a Liberal government completed the structure by establishing District and Parish Councils (1894). The people, in their town, county, or village communities, had been endowed once more with the long-lost power of controlling their own affairs.

Political freedom needs more than the mere machinery of self-government. It needs a just system of law and an efficient judiciary. It got both from Liberalism, which revised the penal code, and made it humane; reconstructed the commercial code, and adapted it to the needs of growing industry; and, finally, reorganized the whole judicial system. Religious disabilities were swept away. The Press, without which political democracy is all but impossible, was freed from all restrictions save those of the libel law, and relieved of the special taxation which had been deliberately imposed to hamper its development.

All these are achievements of a kind which even its bitterest critics are ready to credit to Liberalism: they are all a necessary part of the establishment of political democracy, which is sometimes held to have been the main achievement of Liberalism. But the belief of Liberalism in self-government has gone further than all this. Not the least of its achievements has been the emancipation of trade unions from the restrictions which were imposed upon them, and their equipment with the powers which make them to-day such formidable factors in the life of the nation.

In the period of Tory ascendancy during the French Revolutionary Wars, the formation of combinations among workmen had been absolutely forbidden, under ferocious penalties. Two Radicals, Place and Hume, were mainly responsible for the withdrawal of this restriction in 1824–5; and the Trade Union movement began. But it was not until about 1851 that the trade unions began to organize themselves on a national scale. The strength of the new bodies alarmed the employers, who discovered that they could strike at the unions by prosecuting them for conspiracy in restraint of trade. A Liberal Act of 1871 saved the unions from this danger, though it had to be supplemented by a Conservative Act in 1875. A generation later, the unions found themselves hampered by another difficulty; under the Taff Vale judgment they were held liable for damage done by their members during a strike. The Liberal government of 1906 cancelled this judgment by a Trade Disputes Act which put the trade unions in a position of extraordinary strength and privilege. All the later developments of their power have been made possible by this series of Acts. It is not too much to say that, by giving complete freedom to workmen to organize themselves for common purposes, Liberalism has not only given scope to one form of self-government, but has made bargaining on equal terms possible between employers and employed, and laid the foundations on which a system of co-operative regulation of the conditions of industry may be constructed.

V. IN PUBLIC HEALTH AND EDUCATION

The achievements already enumerated are mainly political in character, and represent rather the removal of restrictions on the freedom of individual action than the positive creation of favourable conditions for the cultivation of individual powers. So far, therefore, we have said nothing which contradicts the widely disseminated notion that Liberalism has never been enthusiastic about constructive social reform. Let us see whether there is any real foundation for this notion.

We saw in an earlier part of this book that before the citizen can be genuinely free he must be helped to win the mastery of his own physical and mental powers ; and this, in the conditions of our civilization, he cannot do without communal aid. What has Liberalism done to give him this aid ?

In the first place, the material conditions of town-life, which were ruinous to the manhood of the nation before the period of Liberal legislation began, have been immeasurably improved by the work of the municipalities (which Liberalism created) acting under powers conferred upon them by a long series of public and private Acts. But this is not all. The creation of an organized system of Public Health regulation was begun by a Liberal Act of 1848, which has been followed by a long series of detailed measures. We take for granted the work which has been done under these Acts by health committees and medical officers in every part of the country, but it is important to remember that it was Liberalism which first insisted that the creation of healthy physical conditions must be assumed as a public obligation. Other measures dealt, in a more or less tentative way, with the problem of housing, and empowered public authorities to demolish unhealthy houses and in some cases to erect better ones. Some of these laws were enacted by Conservative governments. But the impetus came from Liberalism, and the crown of the whole system was the great Housing and Town-planning Act, passed by the Liberal government of 1905–1915. This beneficent measure not only made public authorities responsible for seeing that housing accommodation was healthy and adequate, but imposed upon them the duty of controlling the development of towns in accordance with a systematic plan. This opened, for the first time, the possibility of a really scientific treatment of the problem of the slums—a work which had scarcely begun when it was interrupted by the Great War. There is a vast deal still to be done in this sphere. But no one who has any knowledge of the conditions which existed in British towns eighty years ago can fail to recognize that real and solid progress has already been made. What has made it possible has been, in the main, Liberal legislation.

Yet more important than Public Health for the creation of the conditions of freedom is Education. When Liberalism began its work there was no public provision of education. The first beginnings in the creation of a State system were due to the first Liberal government, which made the first modest grants from public funds in support of schools, and appointed inspectors to supervise their work. It is surely unnecessary to remind any reader that the real foundations of the national system were laid by the Act of 1870, which was passed, amid furious controversy, by Gladstone's first ministry. Much has been done since that date to develop the system, and both of the old political parties have a claim to share the credit. But if to-day every British child is assured of at least so much training as will place in his hands the keys of knowledge, the credit of this achievement belongs to Liberalism. Just as it was Liberalism which insisted that the community must assume the responsibility of securing the conditions of physical health, so it was Liberalism which insisted that the community must assume the responsibility of seeing that no citizen was left in utter ignorance. Here, again, much remains to be done; but the foundations have been well and truly laid.

It may assuredly, therefore, be claimed that the past work of Liberalism is not inconsistent in this sphere with the ideals we have defined; but that, on the contrary, it looks directly towards the kind of programme of action we have contemplated.

VI. IN INDUSTRIAL ORGANIZATION

It is in the sphere of industrial organization, however, that Liberalism is commonly regarded as having been inactive. Many even among those who would be most ready to recognize the value and range of the Liberal achievements in foreign and imperial policy, in the introduction of political democracy, and in the organization of national provision for health and education, would go on to say that in the industrial sphere the cardinal principle of Liberalism had been non-intervention or *laissez-faire*; that it had done little or nothing for the protection of the mass of workers, apart from giving them license to organize themselves in trade unions and to fight out questions of wages and the conditions of labour with the employers; that it had consistently opposed the intervention of the State in industrial matters; and that, in short, its historic policy in this sphere might fairly be summed up as "a free field and no favour, and devil take the hindmost."

Undoubtedly this is a very commonly accepted view of what Liberalism has meant in the industrial sphere. And it is true that there has always been an element in the Liberal party which has regarded with deep-rooted suspicion every measure involving State interference with industry as an invasion of liberty. This element has sometimes been very powerful, especially in the middle of the nineteenth century, when it counted among its supporters the great names of Cobden and Bright. Nevertheless the view which identifies Liberalism with *laissez-faire* is a false view. Gladstone was speaking the literal truth when he said that *laissez-faire* had never been part of the doctrine of Liberalism. For the unflinching opponents of State action have always been a minority, though at some periods an influential minority, in the Liberal party. It is, indeed, a demonstrable and irrefutable fact that all the most striking interferences of the State in industrial matters which have taken place since the industrial revolution, and which have had as their object the protection of the worker against the exercise of undue power by his employer, have been mainly due to Liberal policy. They have been far more extensive than is generally recognized; and taken all together they have pointed towards just such an ideal as we have attempted to describe in the last chapter of this book.

But when you come to examine these interventions closely, one clear principle emerges. Liberalism has always been loth to interfere in the actual processes of production, or to control or meddle with the business of buying, selling and manufacture. But it has never hesitated to interfere in what we have called the human side of industry, or to insist upon the fixing of fair wages and of reasonable hours and conditions of labour. In other words, it has hesitated to interfere where interference involved a restriction of healthy enterprise, but not where interference was necessary for the purpose of securing justice or more real freedom for the worker. It has held that the function of the State is not to control or conduct the processes of production, but to supervise and regulate the conditions under which these processes are to be carried on, in the interests of the community as a whole, and especially of the workers engaged in them.

The most remarkable instances of State interference with industry have been provided by the long code of Factory Acts and Mines Acts, which fixed the age at which children could be employed, defined the maximum hours of regular work in one industry after another, forbade payments in kind, and other unfair devices of the employers, and imposed stringent conditions as to health and safety. A large part of the credit for this remarkable code (which has been carried further than in any other country) has often been given to the Tories, mainly because, in the early days, a great Tory philanthropist, Lord Shaftesbury, was one of the most persistent advocates of this kind of legislation. But two broad facts forbid the acceptance of this view. In the first place from the great Act of 1833 onwards, nearly all the Factory Acts of the nineteenth century were passed by Liberal governments through parliaments which had large Liberal majorities. They were passed, it is true, against the opposition of the small but influential group of *laissez-faire* Liberals ; but they always had Liberal majorities in their favour. And, in the second place, it was Liberal policy which invented the device whereby these Acts were made effective. The earliest Factory Acts were of no avail because the enforcement of them was left to the ordinary machinery of the law, which was impotent to deal with factory conditions; and when Lord Shaftesbury took up the question in 1833 he had no other method to propose. But the Liberal government (which had just abolished slavery) took over Shaftesbury's Bill, and not only carried it through a parliament which had an immense Liberal majority, but made it effective by appointing a number of government inspectors to visit the factories and see that it was obeyed. It was the factory inspectors who made factory laws operative; and it was their reports which led to the steady enlargement of the code. Conservative ministries and parliaments contributed, from time to time, to the work. But in the main the factory code was a Liberal achievement; and to Liberalism must be mainly attributed the assumption by the State of the responsibility of ensuring that those who are engaged in producing the nation's wealth shall not be compelled to work for too long hours or in unhealthy conditions. To appreciate how immense a contribution was thus made to the well-being of the working population, the reader must turn to the reports of the early Commissions whose investigations led to the first Factory and Mines Acts. They will show that, though we are still far from the ideal, we have made an enormous and solid advance on the conditions which existed ninety years ago.

Almost as valuable as the factory code has been the lesser series of laws whereby employers have been made liable for accidents to their work-people. It was a Liberal Act of 1880 which initiated this mode of protecting the workers; and it was a Liberal Act of 1906 which filled in and completed the code.

Nor has Liberalism been content with provisions for the protection of the workers. It defined the conditions under which trading companies should work in a series of Companies Acts. It regulated the work of the banks, by a series of Acts which led the way to Peel's Act of 1844. It has not hesitated to deal drastically with the management of those public services which are necessarily monopolistic in character, taking first the telegraphs and then the telephones under the direct control of the State, and subjecting the railways to a detailed system of regulation, which included the fixing of rates and fares. It was, indeed, the greatest of Liberal statesmen, Gladstone, who came forward, as early as 1844, as the first advocate of the nationalization of the railways. These measures show that in resisting general projects of nationalization Liberalism is not actuated by any doctrinaire objection to State control as such, but solely by the conviction that (except in the case of monopolistic public services) private enterprise ensures greater elasticity, inventiveness and alertness than official management. It has given the warmest support to co-operative enterprises. It invented and applied the method of placing great public services such as dock estates under the management of public trusts which do not earn profits. It has encouraged the development of municipal enterprise by many Acts. In short, it has shown that it believes in the utmost variety of method in the organization of industry; and, far from being committed to any rigid adherence to *laissez-faire*, it has always been ready to use the power of the State for the reorganization of any enterprise necessary to the public welfare in the conduct of which private enterprise seemed to be unable to yield the best results.

In regard to the fixing of wages, and the distribution of the product of industry between employers and employed, Liberalism was throughout the nineteenth century content to trust to collective bargaining on the part of trade unions and employers, in the belief that this was likely to lead to the best results. For a long time this belief (which was strongly held by the trade unions), seemed to be justified. But in the early years of the twentieth century it began to appear that collective bargaining was in many cases insufficient, and that the workers were not likely to get all that industry was capable of yielding them, or to be provided with that degree of security without which freedom must remain unreal, unless the State intervened more directly than it had hitherto done, especially in those trades which were weakly organized. Accordingly, the Liberal government of 1905 entered upon a far-reaching programme of social and industrial reform far ahead of anything that had yet been attempted in any country in the world.

The most remarkable feature of this policy was the institution of Trade Boards, wherein representatives of employers and employed in various unorganized trades were empowered, in conjunction with impartial outsiders, to fix minimum wage rates, which were made legally enforcible. This was the beginning of a system of organized co-operation between the two sides in industry, under the ægis of the State, to which there had hitherto been no parallel. It embodies a principle which may have great consequences; and the party which invented and applied this principle cannot, with any semblance of truth, be described as wedded to the doctrine of *laissez-faire*. With this may be united the establishment of Labour Exchanges in every part of the country to facilitate the fitting of unemployed men into available jobs. The system has been much criticized; but it helped to decasualize some casual trades, such as that of dock labour, and it is capable of many useful applications.

Yet more important than these measures was a systematic and many-sided attempt to deal with the insecurity which haunts the lives of working people. A State system of old-age pensions, a system of insurance against sickness, and the beginning of a system of compulsory insurance against unemployment marked the opening of a new era in the relations of the State to industry. No modern community has ever gone so far as Britain did when she accepted these measures from Liberalism, in the task of building up a sound foundation for the freedom of the whole working population. Unhappily the Great War broke out just at the moment when the new methods were being brought into working order. The terrible ruin and the dislocation of trade which it caused have prevented the full scope and value of these measures from being appreciated; yet, without them, we should have been in a much worse plight to-day.

We have touched upon only the more outstanding of the many measures of social and industrial reform for which Liberalism had been responsible. Many other proposals devised for the protection and well-being of workers, the old and the young, might be enumerated, notably the first attempts to deal with the great problem of the land, on which something had already been done when the war broke out, and which would have been the main task of constructive Liberalism in 1914 and the following years, if the war could have been avoided.

But enough has been said to show how absurd and baseless is the assertion that Liberalism has in any sense or at any time been identified with mere *laissez-faire*. Except in the sphere of monopolistic social services it has, as we have seen, been loth to meddle with the actual conduct of industrial concerns; and it has always and consistently repudiated the Socialist theory that all industrial activities should be brought under the direct ownership and control of the State, because it believes that this would inevitably lead to stagnation and impoverishment. But on the human side of industry—on all questions affecting the life and happiness of the worker—Liberalism has always been ready to use the organized power of the community for the purpose of removing abuses of power and securing justice. Ever since 1833, when the first Liberal ministry was responsible for the first successful Factory Act, Liberalism has accepted the obligation of using all legitimate means to ensure that honest workers shall be secure of healthy conditions of work, reasonable hours, fair wages, just treatment, and that degree of security which is necessary for full freedom. On this side of industrial politics there is, in the Liberal view, only one limitation to the interventions of the State: it must not choke the channels of free and life-giving enterprise legitimately carried on.

Any honest and serious student of the nineteenth century who will take the trouble to review the course and character of Liberal action in the industrial field will, indeed, be driven to two irresistible conclusions. The first is that, though the task is still far from completed, Liberalism has already done vastly more than is generally realized to improve the conditions of life and work of the mass of the population, and to impose upon the directors of industry strict and far-reaching regulations in the interest of the workers. And the second conclusion is that as it has moved forward in its unending aspiration after a larger liberty, the ideal of Liberalism has become more clear and more generous. That ideal, as it is conceived by most progressive Liberals to-day, we have already tried to sketch. In all its main features, it is no novel invention : it is the natural outcome and development of what Liberalism has already done in the past.

VII. IN NATIONAL FINANCE

It is unnecessary to dwell, further than we have already done, upon the achievements of Liberalism in the sphere of local government. Enough to say that the whole system, as it exists to-day, is mainly the result of Liberal statesmanship ; and the further expansion of this form of self-government, which we have indicated as necessary, is only the natural sequel to what has been already achieved.

But something must be said about the work of Liberalism in the sphere of national finance. A hundred years ago, almost the whole burden was thrown upon indirect taxation, which always weighs with especial severity upon the poorer classes. Almost everything which men ate or wore, and their houses, and their very windows, were taxed, while the rich escaped very lightly. And it should be remembered that the burden was relatively almost as heavy then as it is to-day, for if the National Debt is ten times greater to-day than it was a hundred years ago, the nation's power of creating wealth is more than ten times greater. In return for this heavy burden, the taxpayer received far fewer direct services than he does to-day. There was no efficient police system, practically no sanitation, no public system of education, no provision against unemployment other than the Poor Law, no provision against old age or sickness, no protection for child-life, no supervision of industrial conditions, no such amenities as the public libraries, galleries of art, parks and recreation grounds, which to-day place within the reach of poor men opportunities such as many rich men could not reach a hundred years ago. All these services are now rendered by the community to all its members. And the cost of rendering them, as well as the cost of performing other State functions, has been redistributed in such a way that the burden falls mainly upon the well-to-do and only in a minor degree upon the poor. This has been the result of Liberal finance, and it is important that the magnitude of the change which Liberalism has brought about in this respect should be appreciated.

Consider the distribution of our heavy burden of taxation to-day as it is shown by the Budget of 1922–3. There are about 7,000,000 families which do not pay income-tax, and about 3,000,000 which do pay it. The 7,000,000 families only pay indirect taxes on such articles as tea and sugar, beer, spirits, and tobacco ; the 3,000,000 families pay these taxes, and also other indirect taxes, such as those imposed on motor-cars and petrol, but they also pay practically all the direct taxes—income-tax and super-tax, death duties, corporation profits tax, and so forth. Out of a total of £729,000,000 raised by taxation only £270,000,000 was raised by Customs and Excise, which cover all the taxes paid by the 7,000,000 families as well as a substantial (but unknown) amount paid by the 3,000,000. Most of the money thus raised comes back to the taxpayer, especially of the poorer classes, in the form of education, old age pensions, military pensions, health and insurance benefits, and other public services. But the 3,000,000 more fortunate families have to pay, in addition to their share of indirect taxation, more than £400,000,000 of direct taxes. And these in their turn are graduated according to the wealth of the taxpayer, so that a very rich man will have to pay out more than half of his total income every year before he begins to meet the other charges which fall upon him as well as upon other citizens, while, when he dies, nearly half of his fortune will be taken by the State. It may be said that this transfer of the national burdens from the poorer to the richer classes ought to be carried much further. There is a good deal to be said on both sides of that question. But the important thing is to realize how far the transfer has already been carried. It has been carried very much further than in any other civilized State. This readjustment has perhaps alone enabled us to bear the heavy load of post-war finance, and has put Britain in the position of being the only European belligerent power which is paying its way. And these results have been entirely due to the financial policy which was gradually wrought out by Liberalism during the eighty years preceding the Great War.

The greatest of the innovations in public finance whereby these remarkable results were achieved was the establishment of Free Trade, which abolished the taxes on all imported goods with a very few exceptions, such as sugar, tea, and tobacco (which are wholly imported), and beer and spirits (on which internal duties are imposed equivalent to the import duties). Every penny of the duties imposed on these goods comes into the national exchequer ; whereas the old duties, which used to be imposed on foodstuffs and manufactured articles, not only raised the price of the imported goods, but raised the price of the untaxed home products, so that the purchasers paid far more, as a result of the taxes, than came into the exchequer. The old system of taxation (which Liberalism has abolished in Britain, but which still survives in other countries) thus not only imposed the main weight of the national burdens upon the whole body of consumers, and therefore mainly on the poor, it also forced the consumers to pay in increased prices a very much larger sum than was taken for national purposes, and the balance largely went into the pockets of the rich. For nearly seventy years Free Trade has been the central and cardinal principle of Liberal finance, and it is impossible to exaggerate the benefits which it has conferred upon the whole community, but especially upon the poor.

But if the main burden was to be removed from indirect taxation, it was necessary to develop direct taxation in its place. Hence the income-tax became more and more clearly the pivot of Liberal finance. This could only happen gradually, because it took a long time to work out a fair and efficient system of assessing and collecting taxes on income: that is why countries such as France, which have tried to introduce the system suddenly, have found that it has broken down. It was only by degrees that the system was wrought out, and the introduction of a real graduation, whereby rich men pay at a progressively higher rate than men with moderate incomes, was only achieved by the Liberal government just before the war. War necessities led to a rapid development, with the result that we now have an elaborate system of graduation, rising from 1*d*. in the pound on the lowest taxed income up to over 11*s*. in the pound on the largest incomes. But this development was only made possible by the gradual perfecting of the machinery of collection which had been carried out during the previous generation.

A third great innovation of Liberal finance was the imposition of heavy death duties on large fortunes, on a graduated scale. The most striking step in this direction was taken by the Liberal government of

1892–5; and Sir William Harcourt's Budget of 1894, which carried it out, was received with clamorous denunciation by the Conservative party. Nevertheless this system of taxation has undergone great expansion since 1894, and it is capable of still further development. It provides an invaluable means not only of raising revenue without burdening the mass of the people, but of checking the accumulation of great fortunes. The State now takes nearly half of very large fortunes on the death of their possessors; and the principle has been established that the community has a right to take heavy toll of wealth which could only have been made under the conditions of security and prosperity, created by the general activities of the community.

A fourth great innovation in national finance was only beginning to be explored by Liberalism when the war came to interrupt its constructive labours. This is the redistribution of burdens between those who own land and those who occupy and use it. The problem is no easy one. It cannot be solved by facile phrases. But its solution is one of the immediate tasks which lie before Liberalism. When it is solved, it may open up a new source of revenue which will lighten the burdens of the mass of the people. But it is easy to exaggerate the results which can be obtained in this direction, and perhaps the most valuable consequence of a new system of land taxation would be its effect in making land more accessible, and in throwing upon its owners the onus of putting it to the best use.

None of the achievements of Liberalism has been more striking than its success in redistributing the burden of taxation, and in creating a system which has enabled the nation to carry a load such as no other European country could bear. In this respect, as fully as in any other, the work of Liberalism in the past has laid a sound foundation for the labours of the future.

VIII. CONCLUSION

It is but a cursory review which we have been able to take of the work of ninety strenuous years, more full of reforming activity than any other period of equal length in our history. The purpose of this survey has not been merely to put forward a claim to gratitude on behalf of the Liberal party, still less to suggest that Liberalism is entitled to rest on its laurels. Our primary purpose has been to show that the past record of Liberalism is in accord with the analysis of the Liberal ideal which we tried to set forth in the previous chapter ; and that the necessary foundations have been laid upon which alone the structure of the Liberal State, such as we have described it, can be raised.

In international relations Liberalism has stood, and stands to-day, for the maintenance of national freedom and of organized international co-operation. In imperial affairs Liberalism has been responsible for the transformation of what once was, in the literal sense of the term, an empire into a fellowship of free peoples and a trusteeship on behalf of backward peoples. In the organization of the nation's political activities it has stood for the fullest possible extension of self-government, giving the management of common affairs in each case to those who are most directly concerned, trusting to persuasion rather than to force as the best mode of settling differences, and enthroning above all the sovereignty of the community. It has insisted that the community must assume the responsibility for providing every citizen with the means of becoming master of his own powers of body and mind. In industrial matters, while maintaining that the enterprise and inventiveness of individuals must be given the freest vent as the main driving force of progress, it has also asserted the right and duty of the community to interfere in all those aspects of industrial organization which affect the life and happiness of the workers, and has striven, not altogether in vain, to secure for them freedom of combination, reasonable hours and conditions of work, and a fair share of the product of their toil. In the distribution of national burdens it has brought about a great transference of loads from weaker to stronger shoulders, and has succeeded, in a degree unparalleled in any other country, in graduating taxation according to the ability of the payer to bear it.

In all these spheres the progress which it has made has been steady and (as human affairs go) rapid. The task is as yet only half achieved, and the next stages of progress will be rendered tenfold more arduous by the difficulties which have been created by the war. Nevertheless the true lines of advance have been pretty clearly laid down. The ideal, as clearly conceived as is practicable in the unending flux and change of human affairs, stands before us. It cannot be attained in a moment. But it is possible to mark out the next steps which should be taken; and this we shall attempt to do in the following chapter.

For fuller detail about the nineteenth century, read Trevelyan's "British History in the Nineteenth Century," or Ramsay Muir's "Short History of the British Commonwealth," Vol. II, especially Bk. IX, Chaps. ii, viii, x; Bk. X, Chaps. iii, iv, viii, ix; Bk. XI, Chap. vi, and Bk. XII, Chap. ii. Gladstone's famous West Calder speech on the principles of foreign policy will be found in a collection of speeches on foreign policy published in the World's Classics. The change in imperial policy is traced in Muir's "Expansion of Europe." One aspect of Liberal social policy may be traced in Hutchins & Harrison's "History of Factory Legislation." Fuller lists of books on special subjects will be found in Muir's "British Commonwealth."

CHAPTER IV

THE IMMEDIATE TASKS OF REFORM

WE have sketched the aims which progressive Liberals set before themselves, not as an ultimate ideal for humanity, but as a better order of things capable of being shaped by human endeavour out of existing conditions in a reasonable space of time. We have shown that these aims are in accord with the record and traditions of Liberalism, and that in many aspects a substantial advance has already been made towards their realization. It remains to consider what are the immediate steps which a Liberal party ought to advocate, in the conditions of to-day, in order that we may go forward as rapidly as possible in the building of a happier order on the foundations already laid: what policy or programme it ought to put forward when it invites the support of the electorate.

Great reforms are urgently needed in many spheres; and as all the aspects of politics are closely inter-related, it is impossible to lay down a clear order of priority. Many hold, for example, that industrial reorganization is the first and greatest of our needs. But the possibility of success in any such reorganization must largely depend upon a revival of trade, which in its turn depends upon the restoration of peaceful conditions and productive activity throughout the world; and that can only be forwarded by a wise foreign policy. Even more vital to an industrial revival is a wise handling of national finance, which in its turn is largely dependent upon the possibility of reducing unproductive expenditure on armaments —once more a question of foreign policy. Again, the practicability of industrial reorganization, and the forms which it is to assume, must depend very largely upon the efficiency of our machinery of government, which is manifestly in disrepair and no longer commands the full confidence of the nation.

Even those who share the writer's conviction that the problems of social and industrial reorganization are the most vital and important problems of the future must therefore recognize that they must be considered along with the other problems we have named; and that reforming activity will have to go on concurrently in all these spheres. But there are some problems bequeathed to us by the war, which insistently claim priority of consideration; and we shall first deal with the problems of foreign relations, and with the economic difficulties left by the war, before turning to deal with the larger projects of reform which Liberalism ought to undertake.

I. THE EUROPEAN SITUATION

Europe is in a desperate plight, and unless it can be restored to a condition of economic health there is little prospect that we in Britain will see prosperity for a long time to come, or be able to secure well-being for our people. There are some who say that we ought to wash our hands of the European imbroglio, and return to the discarded policy of "splendid isolation." We cannot do this, even if we would. For good or ill, we are a part of Europe; we prosper with its prosperity, or suffer with its ruin. It is both our duty and our interest to do all that we can to help in its restoration. What can we do?

It is not only the exhaustion and impoverishment caused by the war and the upheavals produced by a complicated and ill-devised peace settlement which have reduced Europe to economic chaos; these are serious enough, but they can be overcome, given favourable conditions. The gravest difficulties arise from a universal sense of insecurity, which has brought it about that, in spite of the compulsory reduction of the German army, the bankrupt nations are maintaining military forces on so great a scale that there are actually more armed men in Europe to-day than there were in 1913. It is not because they want war that the nations are pursuing this policy; it is because they dread war, have seen its results, and, being full of mutual suspicions, are determined to be ready to resist attack, or to assert their "rights" by force. The cost of these huge armies makes it impossible for them to balance their budgets; they have to resort to the disastrous device of printing money; and depreciating currencies and wildly fluctuating exchanges make a restoration of trade all but impossible and intensify the difficulties. There can be no cure for this state of things until the sense of insecurity is banished. If that could be done, the purely economic problem is by no means insoluble.

The difficulties arising from the problems of German reparations and inter-allied debts, when closely examined, are only the most outstanding illustrations of this general difficulty. It is absolutely just that Germany should be made to pay the maximum practicable sum towards the repair of the ruin she caused. It would be absolutely just that Germany should be compelled to bring all the dead to life—if it were possible. But to demand the impossible, and to clog the wheels of industry until the impossible is performed, can only lead to ruin. If the politicians would agree, it is quite possible to fix, on a scientific basis, the maximum amount that Germany can pay without ruinously dislocating the course of trade. But in fixing this amount two things have to be remembered. The first is that Germany can only pay when she is in a position to earn; and her position to-day is much worse than it was four years ago. The second is that Germany's vast industrial machine is one of the pivots of world trade, and until it is restored to smooth working order the currents of world trade cannot flow freely.

Why has not an adjustment on these lines been reached long ago? The main obstacle is the policy of France, who is able to insist upon the exact fulfilment of an impossible treaty to which our honour was unhappily pledged. Why does France adopt this policy, which may lead to the final collapse of the European economic system? Her statesmen know that Germany cannot pay, until she is restored to economic health. But they dread her restoration even more than they desire her payments. If they cannot get full reparation, at least (they think) they can use the reparations claim to ruin Germany and make her impotent for harm. Not France only but Belgium, Italy, and Poland are haunted by the dread of what a revived Germany might do; and are therefore tempted to pursue a policy which threatens Europe with early bankruptcy, and with a grim vista of unrest and wars of revenge. Thus it is the sense of insecurity which lies at the root of the reparations problem; and there will be no solution until this is recognized.

The League of Nations was constituted precisely for

the purpose of giving to all peoples a sense of security, by making them feel that each was protected by all. Manifestly it has failed to do so, by the means which it has hitherto been able to employ. The reason why it has failed is that the obligations of mutual protection which it imposes are too general to give confidence to a generation that is haunted by the hatreds of war. The promise of assistance against sudden attack which it holds out is vague and contingent. France can feel no security in an undertaking which commits nobody to immediate action, and which binds Siam and the Argentine in exactly the same degree as it binds Britain and Italy; for what is everybody's business is apt to be nobody's business.

Belief in the League of Nations as a substitute for swollen armaments and rival alliances is the very pivot of Liberal foreign policy. But the difficulty described in the last paragraph must be frankly faced if the League is to be made a reality. How can this difficulty be overcome? It can be overcome if any nation which feels itself insecure is enabled to make definite agreements for mutual defence with other nations. But this, by itself, would merely be a return to the old system of rival alliances, which brought on the war. In order to prevent so unhappy a development, (1) such defensive agreements must be communicated to and published by the League of Nations and be subject to its criticism; and (2) it must be defined that they only become operative if or when an aggressive power has failed to utilize the methods of judicial inquiry, arbitration, and delay which the League provides, or (should these steps have been taken) if the Council of the League decides by a majority that an act of aggression has been committed. Thus safeguarded and brought into harmony with the system of the League, defensive agreements and treaties would not be a return to the old and bad system which continually menaced Europe with war; they would form essential means of strengthening the League and fulfilling its aims. They would create a sense of security, and make disarmament possible; and this would lead to the balancing of budgets, the stabilizing of exchanges, and the revival of trade.

M. Poincaré has stated publicly that he would accept an agreement under the League as a guarantee of France's security. Britain ought to be ready to be a party to such an agreement with France, perhaps along with Italy and Belgium, provided that the conclusion of the agreement were made part of a general settlement of reparations and inter-allied debts; and in order that a final settlement may be reached, without which no full revival of trade will be possible, Britain ought to be ready to forgo wholly or in part her claim to a share of reparations and to the repayment of the debts nominally due to her, provided that these concessions are accompanied by the adoption of a scheme of progressive disarmament and by a balancing of the budgets of the Powers which profit by them.

It is only on the basis of some guarantee of security, some real safeguard against wars of revenge, that any settlement of the troubles of Europe can be reached. This is the crucial fact upon which France has insisted, and to which British statesmanship has been obstinately blind. The economic problems are not incapable of solution, once the problem of security has been satisfactorily solved. But we must set our faces against one-sided or exclusive agreements. If Germany should become a member of the League of Nations, and should then claim a guarantee of her own security, we ought to be ready to make with her just such an agreement for defence against aggression as we make with France, provided that Germany accepts an impartial settlement of the reparations claim, and honestly sets to work to satisfy it.

In brief, the policy which Liberalism ought to pursue—and which, it would appear, only Liberalism is likely to pursue—may be set out in summary as follows:—

(1) To aim at restoring a sense of security in Europe, as the foundation of political and economic health; and to do this by encouraging the formation, under the League of Nations, of a series of regional agreements for mutual defence which would only become operative under such conditions as the League would define.

(2) To be ready to become a party to such agreements, in the first instance with France, as a part of a general settlement of outstanding difficulties, but later also with Germany and with any other Powers to whom it is important that a British guarantee should be given.

(3) To secure as a condition of these agreements that the maximum amount of reparations which Germany can pay within a reasonable period should be fixed by an impartial body of experts appointed by the League of Nations.

(4) Since the figure thus fixed would certainly be insufficient to satisfy all the expectations of 1919, Britain must be ready to safeguard France and Belgium, the chief sufferers during the war, against undue sacrifices (*a*) by forgoing or postponing her own claim to a share of the reparations payments, and (*b*) by a frank cancellation of inter-allied debts, which are in any event practically irrecoverable, and the claim to which only adds to the confusion of European finance and the difficulty of restoring trade.

This would leave Britain still burdened with the debt to America, which was mainly incurred on behalf of our European allies; and it would mean that, in appearance at all events, Britain would have to bear a wholly disproportionate share of the cost of the war. This is the price we should have to pay for release from the obligations of a ruinous treaty. But it should not be forgotten that we have already attained a real measure of security by the sinking of the German fleet, and a real contribution to reparations in the transfer to us of a large part of the German mercantile marine. The debt to America will in any case have to be paid, since she insists upon it, and we are not going to be false to our obligations, whatever other nations may do. Nothing is gained by insisting upon the debts due to us from our European allies, because they cannot be paid; they only stand in the way of a restoration of economic health in Europe, and we shall gain far more by the revival of trade than we could ever conceivably gain by insisting upon keeping unpayable debts on paper, and so preventing the economic restoration of the world.

In substance this is the policy which has been advocated during the last two years by the Liberal leaders, Mr. Asquith and Lord Grey. So far as reparations and debts are concerned, they have gradually brought almost all responsible opinion round to their view, which is now adopted even by those who framed or accepted the Treaty of Versailles. But the essential feature—the very foundation—of this policy is the recognition of the necessity of security as a condition precedent to any lasting settlement. It is the failure to recognize this which has led to the unhappy breach between France and Britain. But it is not enough to recognize the need for security. The mode in which security is to be obtained must not involve separate or exclusive alliances. It must not disregard the League of Nations (as one proposal of this kind did), but must treat the League as its pivot. And it is because it does this that the policy we have described represents the only way of solving the troubles of Europe which is compatible with Liberal ideals.

II. THE FINANCIAL OUTLOOK

The second fundamental problem of to-day is that of national finance. In the present year (1922–3) the Budget estimates show that we are to raise about £910,000,000 (of which £729,000,000 will be raised by taxation) as compared with less than £200,000,000 before the war. This represents a burden of taxation averaging something like £73 a year for every family in the country. Britain is the most heavily taxed country in the world, and it is the only one of the belligerent countries (except America) which is paying its way. It is significant that of this vast total a good deal more than half—£563,000,000—represents the cost of past wars and of preparation for future wars. Manifestly the security of the world's peace is the foundation of national health, in finance as in other respects; and a wise foreign policy is the first condition of well-being.

How are we to bear this colossal burden? How can we hope to regain prosperity while so large a share of the total wealth which the nation produces (about one-fourth) has to be taken out of the pockets of the citizens and spent by Government, mainly for unproductive purposes? What is the use, in face of these burdens, of advocating large and costly schemes of reform?

Of this vast sum about one-tenth (nearly £90,000,000)

represents pensions to disabled soldiers and the dependents of the dead. This will be a diminishing burden, which will shrink to nothing in the course of a generation or so. But it will not shrink immediately. Indeed, it ought rather to increase, for the duty of providing for those who set their lives between us and ruin is a duty which must be performed in no grudging spirit.

More than one-third of the total (£335,000,000) represents the interest on the National Debt, mainly incurred by the war. There are many people who hold that this is an unjustifiable burden ; that wealth ought to have been conscripted just as life was conscripted in a great national emergency. There is a great deal of justice in this view. But it overlooks three things. In the first place, it was not possible to "conscript" the needful capital, because it was not a case of seizing something that was already there. Most of the existing capital in 1914 was sunk in mills and other unrealizable forms, and the capital that was needed had to be created, in the only way in which capital *can* be created—by saving. No amount of force could have compelled people to save a sufficient amount of their earnings : they had to be persuaded, by the promise of interest. In the second place, a large proportion of the money was provided by banks and insurance companies out of the premiums or deposits of their customers, on which they had to earn interest if they were to fulfil their obligations ; and if these holdings were cancelled, widespread ruin would result. In the third place, it would be monstrously unjust to penalize those who lent their savings to the State in its time of need, while leaving untouched those who were at the same time putting their money in profitable enterprises. The National Debt has been borrowed on the word of honour of Britain, whether wisely or unwisely. That word cannot be tampered with without destroying the nation's credit.

The bulk of the debt is held by British citizens, and largely by the same citizens who pay the greater part of the income-tax. This leads to the absurd result that we have apparently to maintain an army of tax collectors to levy taxes from the same people to whom another army of officials pay the money back in the form of interest. To meet this situation it has been proposed that we should make a levy on all capital holdings of more than a certain amount, and pay off a part of the National Debt with the proceeds: the debt-holders who were paid off could then, it is argued, re-invest the money in the concerns from which it was withdrawn, so that industry would not be damaged, while the taxes would be reduced by anything up to £200,000,000 a year. This was, substantially, the proposal which the Labour party put forward as the chief item of its programme in the last election; but it was no invention of the Labour party.

There is no inherent injustice in a capital levy. It is confiscation, but so is any other form of taxation; and the only question for statesmanship, as in the case of any other tax, is the question whether, on balance, this particular form of confiscation is advantageous or not. Now a capital levy is unquestionably exposed to certain real dangers and difficulties. It creates alarm and a sense of insecurity among investors; how dangerous this may be was shown by the way in which owners of capital in Switzerland hastened to invest it in other countries when in 1922 it was merely proposed to introduce a capital levy. Again, it is extraordinarily difficult to assess the value of capital justly, especially in a time of fluctuating prices. What is the value, for example, of a nominal £10,000 in a reconstructed cotton mill which is paying no dividends owing to bad trade? And finally, nearly all capital (apart from the national and other public debts) is invested in industry. To withdraw it may lead to infinite complications, even if it were certain to be replaced; and of course there could be no certainty that the holders of National Debt, when paid off, would reinvest their money in the precise concerns from which money had been withdrawn.

These are real difficulties. Nevertheless, in favourable circumstances, they could in theory be overcome. Such circumstances existed, in the judgment of many Liberals, immediately after the war, in 1919 and 1920. Everybody then recognized that heroic measures had to be taken to restore healthy conditions after the waste of war, and this feeling would have partly balanced the alarm caused by the levy. War fortunes (which have since been largely dissipated) were still intact. There was a boom in trade, which would have made it easier for capitalists to pay the levy, would have encouraged banks to give them advances where necessary, and would have made it likely that the holders of debt, when paid off, would re-invest their money in British industrial concerns. If the levy had checked the boom, that might not have been a bad thing. If ever a capital levy could have been carried out, that was the moment; and therefore many Liberals (including the present writer) were strong advocates of a capital levy *at that time*.

But the moment passed, and it is more than doubtful if it will ever return. The boom was succeeded by the worst period of trade depression we have ever known. Much of the invested capital of the country (on which the levy would have had to be made) was earning no profits at all. How could its value have been assessed? How could the banks be expected to make advances to the almost bankrupt owners to enable them to pay the levy? The owners could not hand over one-fifth of the bricks and mortar of their mills. They would have had to pay the levy out of their working capital, by means of which they buy materials, pay wages, and keep their works going until their products are ready for sale. They could not expect the paid-off holders of debt to invest their money in concerns that would not pay a dividend. Privately owned concerns would have had to close down, and the already terrible volume of unemployment would have been greatly increased. This was why Liberals who had advocated a capital levy in 1920 opposed it in 1922. They opposed it not because they wished to protect rich men, but because they wished to defend the livelihood of poor men. In advocating a capital levy at such a moment, the Labour party showed that it had no sense of realities, but was carried away by a mere blind desire to mulct the capitalist, without considering consequences.

But if a capital levy is excluded, what hope is there of dealing with the terrible load of debt which drags at our feet like the cannon-balls that used to be tied to the ankles of slaves to prevent their escape? One consoling fact ought not to be forgotten. Our debt to-day is ten times as great as it was a hundred years ago, after the Napoleonic War. But our power of producing wealth is more than ten times as great as it then was. Relatively, therefore, the burden is no greater than our ancestors bore. Now it is true that the old debt was not paid off nearly as fast as it ought to have been and could have been. But the burden it imposed on the people was immensely reduced, partly because the nation worked hard and became richer, but also because when trade became good money became cheap, and it was possible to pay off debt at a high rate of interest with money borrowed at a low rate of interest. If we could raise enough money at 3 per cent to pay off the whole debt (which averages 5 per cent) we should save in the annual burden of interest over £130,000,000 a year. This ought gradually to become possible when trade revives. And that will happen (*a*) when peace is restored in Europe, and (*b*) when the removal of industrial unrest at home makes earning and saving more easy.

But we must not be content with this prospect. We must, as rapidly as possible, remove the dead-weight of debt by paying off the capital. We have ruled out as impracticable (at any rate within any period we can easily foresee) a general levy on capital. But there is one form of levy on capital which is already in use: the death duties, whereby the rich man's fortune is mulcted on a graduated scale when he dies. Can we set apart this capital levy for capital redemption? This would be highly desirable. But at present the £48,000,000 which these taxes yield are needed for annual expenditure. Most Liberals are in favour of a substantial increase of death duties, and they would in theory prefer that the money thus obtained should be set apart for debt redemption. If the death duties could be increased to a figure which would nearly correspond with the sum we now spend on pensions, they could be regarded as being used for what is equivalent to a capital charge; and it might be provided that as the pensions charge decreased, the balance of the yield from death duties should be devoted to debt redemption. This is perhaps as far as we should go. For it should be remembered that in whatever form we make provision for paying off debt—whether by a general capital levy or by the limited capital levy of death duties—this generation will be made to mulct itseif for the advantage of the next. And if it mulcts itseif so severely as to crippie itself, the next generation will not really profit. We have to think of the next generation, we have to make sacrifices for it But perhaps the thought and the sacrifice will best take the form of providing the next generation with healthy conditions and a sound training, rather than that of stinting it of these things in order to reduce its financial burdens; a healthy and well-trained people will be better able to shoulder heavy burdens.

For the present, therefore, we must postpone any immediate and drastic reduction of the debt charge; but we may expect that, when prosperity revives, the burden will be steadily reduced by a reduction of the rate of interest, and that the capital charge will be progressively diminished by repayments out of death duties, especially when the cost of pensions begins to decrease. But can we hope for any early decrease in the burden of taxation, which now weighs upon the industry of the nation with crippling severity? Both of the two main forms of taxation—indirect (or duties on articles of consumption), and direct (or income-tax)—are far too high. An income-tax at 5*s*. in the pound (even when its actual incidence is graded from 1*d*. up to 11*s*. in the pound) hampers industrial development, checks saving, and therefore keeps the rate of interest high and prevents the reduction of debt charge. But still more disastrous is the burden of indirect taxation, which falls upon all classes, but bears with especial severity upon the poor, and (what is worse) taxes large families, irrespective of their income, far more severely than small families. Out of every £1 which the housewife spends on tea, sugar, cocoa, coffee and dried fruits about 6*s*. represents taxation; and this means that in a time of exceptional distress like the present the sufferings of the poorest are intensified. The actual burden on the poorer classes ought to be greatly reduced: it ought to be swept away altogether in the case of those whose incomes are below a reasonable margin of subsistence. There are only two ways in which this can be done without increasing the burdens of the existing income-tax payers to a ruinous extent. One is by reducing expenditure, to which we shall return presently. The other is by transferring the burden that has to be borne by the wage-earning class from indirect to direct taxation. If instead of paying his contribution to the State in the form of duties on tea and sugar, the workingman paid it in a direct tax on his income (above a certain limit) he would have the advantage of exemptions in proportion to the amount of his income and the number of his family, whereas now he is taxed on the size of his family, irrespective of his income. This is a reform in the incidence of taxation which would be altogether beneficial, if it were practicable. But in one way or another it is essential that taxation on articles of universal consumption should be reduced as rapidly as possible.

What can we hope for in the way of reduced expenditure? Undoubtedly savings can be made by watchful economy in all the public departments, by stricter Treasury control and by constant Parliamentary criticism: these are methods upon which Liberalism has always laid the greatest emphasis. But the savings which can be made in these ways will (except in one sphere) at the most amount to a few millions, for large cuts have already been made during the last two years.

On the main items of domestic expenditure we neither can nor ought to make any substantial reductions. We cannot afford to reduce our expenditure on education (£51,000,000): this is only £5 a year for every family, and though there is doubtless some waste in this expenditure, the system is as yet so far from perfect that we must look to an increase rather than a decrease. Nor can we reduce the expenditure on Old Age Pensions (£21,000,000); on the contrary we must abolish the restrictions which at present penalize thrift, and this will involve an increase of some millions. The Labour party, indeed, advocates a reduction of the age limit to 65, which would more than double the cost; but the aim of this reduction would be better secured by a system of insurance worked out upon an industrial basis in connexion with the unemployment and sickness insurance schemes. Finally, we cannot attempt to reduce the expenditure on public health; we must contemplate additional outlay, for some time to come, on housing; and the burden imposed upon the State by unemployment insurance, though it will decrease when trade revives, ought to be increased (as we shall see later) while the acute depression of to-day continues.

Where, then, are we to look for any large decrease of public expenditure? There is only one branch of national finance in which it is possible: the outlay on defence services. In 1913 we spent on military preparations £86,000,000. This was regarded as an appallingly large sum, and its size was due to the competition in armaments in which we were compelled to follow the lead of the continental Powers. Since then the German Fleet has gone to the bottom of the sea, and the German Army has been reduced; but our expenditure is now £138,000,000. The increase as compared with 1913 is covered by the rise in the cost of living. But we ought now to be spending on a much lower scale than in 1913. We shall only be able to do this when a sense of security has been created in Europe, and the European nations have been persuaded to disarm.

It would seem, then, that we cannot look forward to any considerable reduction in the national burdens during the next few years ; and our best hope is that we may be able to increase our wealth, in order to make the burden lighter in that way. But *if* we can bring about real peace in Europe and therefore cut down our military expenditure—*if* we can obtain a real revival of trade and stop the waste that comes from incessant friction between employers and employed—*if* we can encourage saving on such a scale as will reduce the current rate of interest, and so cut down the burden of the debt charge—*if* we can pursue a stringent but wise economy which will not cripple the next generation in the performance of its tasks—we may legitimately look for a real and increasing diminution of our burdens.

Here are many "ifs," and it is obvious that everything depends upon the way in which our finances are managed, and upon the concurrent maintenance of a wise foreign policy and an enlightened and progressive industrial policy. The outlook is bleak enough, but it is best to look the facts in the face, and not to cozen ourselves with promises which cannot be fulfilled. We can do a good deal to ease the adjustment of the burden, to bring about a fairer distribution of the national earnings, to remove or diminish the insecurity that haunts the lives of our people ; on these heads we shall have something to say later. But we cannot by any jugglery get rid of the hard facts about the burden which the nation has to bear ; and if we resort to unsound financial devices we shall make things worse instead of better.

This being so, it is impossible not to deplore the reckless projects which have been put forth by the Labour party. It has not only proposed to cut down the National Debt by one-third or one-half, by means of a capital levy raised at a moment of disastrously bad trade ; it has also proposed an immense immediate increase of our expenditure on objects with which every Liberal sympathizes, but on a scale which is wholly impracticable in present conditions. And, finally, it has proposed an immediate readjustment of the burden of taxation whereby (*a*) ultimately the whole, and immediately a large proportion, of the existing indirect taxes would be cancelled, and (*b*) all incomes below £250 would be exempted from income-tax, and all incomes below £500 largely relieved. The whole cost of these changes would be thrown upon incomes of more than £500. This would mean that the nation would be divided into an untaxed majority of 8,000,000 families, and a minority of 2,000,000 who would be so heavily taxed that they would have no incomes left. It has been calculated —by a hostile critic, it is true—that after the incomes of the taxpaying minority had been practically taxed out of existence, the scheme would leave a deficit of £40,000,000 per annum out of which to meet the immense promises of new expenditure included in the Labour party's programme. This is, no doubt, an exaggeration. But it is not too much to say that the proposals of the Labour party display a reckless irresponsibility in dealing with matters of grave moment which is nothing less than deplorable.

It is possible that the income-tax and super-tax may be further graduated so as to weigh more heavily on the higher grades of income, though already they take from the highest grades over 11s. in the pound. It is possible and highly desirable that indirect taxation may be reduced by the methods we have already indicated. But it is neither possible nor just that four-fifths of the nation, while wielding political sovereignty, should be freed from all financial responsibility for the policy which they support.

There are two further reforms in taxation to which Liberalism is pledged; they will not materially affect the volume of the State's revenue, but they will remove obstacles to the development of trade, and give encouragement to enterprise. The first is the immediate and total repeal of the protective duties and restrictions upon imports imposed during and since the war, including the Safeguarding of Industries Act and the Dyes Act. The amounts which the duties levied under these Acts have yielded to the exchequer are entirely negligible—probably insufficient to pay for the cost of collecting them. But the dislocation of industry which they have caused, the exasperation which they have produced, and the diversion of trade from our shores for which they have been responsible, mark them as futile and mischievous financial measures. The second needed reform is a complete recast of the whole system of rating and taxing land. This would have been one of the earliest undertakings of Liberalism had the war not broken out in 1914; a partial and not very satisfactory beginning had already been made in the Budget of 1909, but this has since been cancelled and the whole problem remains to be dealt with afresh. It will be among the first tasks of Liberalism.

III. THE PROBLEM OF EXCEPTIONAL UNEMPLOYMENT

Before we turn to the tasks of permanent political and social reform to which Liberalism is eager to address itself, there is one more problem of a temporary and exceptional character, due to the general unsettlement of the world, on which something ought to be said. This is the problem of dealing with the abnormal and unprecedented volume of unemployment which now exists. On what may be called "normal" unemployment (which, over a series of years, amounts to about 4 per cent of the working population) we have already said something, and shall have something more to say: it is a problem of manageable dimensions, capable of a reasonable and just solution. But abnormal unemployment, such as we have recently seen (which has reached as high as 15 per cent), must break down any machinery designed for normal conditions. If trade does not recover quickly, this state of things may last for some time, and it is necessary to have an intelligible policy for dealing with it.

It is an agreed starting-point that the unemployed cannot merely be left to starve. As things are, they are partly maintained—very inadequately—by insurance benefits (unjustly and inaccurately described as "doles"); but the insurance funds, having been designed to meet normal needs, are wholly insufficient, even with additional aid from the Treasury, to meet the extraordinary situation of to-day, and they have to be supplemented on a large scale by real "doles" under the Poor Law. The burden thus thrown upon the rates hampers the revival of industry. It also falls with especial severity upon the poorer districts; and it is manifestly wrong that the cost of dealing with a national economic crisis should thus be thrown upon the localities which are already hardest hit. Even so, the unemployed are not adequately maintained; they are undergoing a progressive moral and physical deterioration; and their children are in many cases suffering hardships which may affect the quality of their work and of their citizenship throughout their lives.

Is there no way of avoiding these terrible consequences? Could not the public money now spent both in insurance benefits and in Poor Law doles be more usefully employed in making it possible for work to be undertaken that under the economic circumstances of the moment cannot be undertaken without help? There are some cases in which this is obviously so. We urgently need 500,000 houses: if they were built, and let at reasonable rents, they would be occupied at once; but they are not being built because they cost more than would be covered by the rents their tenants can pay. The margin is, however, not now very wide. On the other hand there are 150,000 builders out of work, who are receiving weekly very large sums in the aggregate, though inadequate sums individually, to maintain them and their families in enforced idleness. It is probable that if the sums thus spent were distributed in subsidies to builders, to enable them to let the houses they build at practicable rents, they would be able to employ the whole 150,000 at full wages, the housing problem would be put in the way of solution, the builders' plant would be profitably utilized, the spending of all these wages in the ordinary course of trade would enlarge the demand for all sorts of goods, and at the end the nation would be enriched by the possession of a large number of houses. The only way in which this could be done would be that the State should compute the amount spent in the maintenance of unemployed builders, and spend that amount in building subsidies. The reason why it is not done is that this would involve an immediate increase of *Treasury* expenditure, while the saving on the rates (which are paid by the same people as pay the taxes) would go into the accounts of local authorities, and would be distributed over so many of them that it would not be very perceptible. But this is not a valid reason for refusing to undertake a wholesome and economically sound enterprise.

There are other instances of national needs which will sooner or later have to be met, which are not now being undertaken because under existing conditions they do not seem to be economically sound, but which *would* seem economically sound if their projectors could draw upon the large sums now being spent upon the maintenance in half-starved idleness of the men whom they would employ. It is the duty of an intelligent government, in a moment of crisis, to find the means of bridging such irrational gulfs between the men who want work and the work that needs to be done: the material for the bridge is at hand in the money that is actually being expended on the maintenance of those who would be employed on such projects. Spent in the manner indicated, these funds would leave the nation richer than before; spent as they are now spent, they leave it poorer, by the deterioration of the men and women who have to live in half-starved idleness. It ought not to be difficult to compute how much could be expended in this way *even without increasing the total demand upon the wealth of the community*; and up to that limit at least, government expenditure would not merely be justified, it would be profitable, even if, for the moment, it seemed to increase the national outgoings.

The undertakings which would satisfy the conditions just set forth would affect only a limited number of industries, but on the whole they would be some of the industries which are suffering most. The increased spending-power of the men thus employed and of their employers would appreciably help to relieve unemployment in other industries, by enlarging the demand for their products. But there would remain a large group of industries which could not be directly helped by this method: the textile trades, for example. In these industries the only available way of minimizing—for that is all that is possible—the evils of a period of exceptional trade depression would be by a system of organized relay-work with partial unemployment benefit, such as was successfully wrought out in the cotton trade during the war. To some extent this method has been applied. But it has been applied only sporadically. It is only possible in a highly organized industry, wherein co-operation between employers and employed is habitual. It would be made possible by such a system of industrial self-government as we have outlined in an earlier part of this book. But alas! this system has yet to be created.

The policy which Liberalism should advocate for dealing with an exceptional crisis such as now faces us would, then, briefly be as follows:

(1) It is the duty of the community to maintain those who are out of work through no fault of their own, and the scale of maintenance should be such as not to involve moral and physical deterioration in the recipients.

(2) It is wasteful to spend the public funds thus necessarily expended, on maintenance-in-idleness. To the utmost possible extent they should be used to make productive work practicable. Therefore the State should be prepared to undertake the granting of subsidies for useful work, up to at least the amount which would otherwise be expended in maintaining those whom this work would employ, from whatever public source this expenditure would come.

(3) It is the duty of the State to encourage the

organization of industries on such a basis as will enable them to deal with such crises as the present by co-operative means.

(4) It is unjust and uneconomical that the burden of dealing with unemployment due to national conditions should be thrown upon the Poor Law areas in which unemployment happens to be most prevalent. The funds expended on exceptional (as distinct from normal) unemployment should be administered as a whole, in a uniform way, so that the burden may be fairly distributed; and this implies that these funds should, in the main, be drawn from national, not local, sources.

IV. EDUCATION AND PUBLIC HEALTH

It is a relief to turn from the difficulties created by the war to the permanent reforms upon which Liberalism would have been engaged if the war had been averted, and which have become all the more necessary because of the troubles that the war has brought.

Some needful reforms, indeed, must necessarily be hampered and delayed by the financial exigencies born of the war. This difficulty will be especially felt in education and public health—the spheres in which the community has definitely assumed responsibility for providing its citizens with the conditions of a healthy and rational life. It will not hamper us, in anything like the same degree, in the task of reforming our political system, or in the still more important task of bringing about a readjustment of the relations between the active factors in industry, capital, management and labour; for these reforms do not necessarily involve any outlay of public funds. Indeed, the very acuteness of the crisis in the nation's fortunes makes it more urgent than ever that these problems should be solved. This is the answer to those who argue that social reforms must be postponed until prosperity returns: social reforms are necessary as a means of restoring prosperity by giving to the nation the strength and unity without which it cannot overcome its difficulties. In those reforms which involve a large outlay from public funds, such as the improvement of our schools and the clearing of our slums, we must be content to advance less rapidly than we should desire. But in those reforms which involve mainly a readjustment of human relationships there is no reason why we should not make rapid progress. And even in education and public health we must not yield to the temptation of throwing up our hands too easily; for if we do, we shall betray the rising generation.

It is nothing less than a disaster that the war burden should have fallen upon the nation at this precise moment. For in the years preceding the war we had just begun to address ourselves, on a large and comprehensive scale, to the creation of a co-ordinated educational system, and to a courageous treatment of the problems of public health. It is, indeed, seldom realized how remarkable was the progress made in these two spheres, during the dozen years which preceded the war, and mainly under the guidance of the Liberal government of those years. The nation was at last equipping itself to face the rivalry of better equipped peoples. And it will be a mere disaster if we allow ourselves to be persuaded that further progress in these fields must be abandoned until we have regained the prosperity which further progress in these fields will alone enable us to regain.

Before the Education Act of 1902, although we had created a national system of elementary education, we had done practically nothing for the higher educational grades ; which was as if we had laid out a system of irrigation with all its pipes and conduits, but had provided no new cisterns or reservoirs wherefrom the pipes and conduits might be fed. After 1902 a national system of secondary schools was rapidly brought into being ; these schools were more or less co-ordinated with the elementary schools ; the vital task of creating an adequate corps of teachers was taken in hand ; and this was made possible, and a very serious gap in the whole system was more or less filled, by the establishment of a series of city universities. No period of British history has seen such rapid educational progress as took place during the dozen years before the war. The system thus swiftly created was full of crudities and defects. The new schools and the new universities had scarcely yet had time to form their characters, and they were in a thousand ways deficient in equipment. They were too uniform in type, too mechanical in method, too much subject to official or bureaucratic control. It may even be true that in some respects they were uneconomically organized. All this was the natural outcome of the circumstances in which they were created. Yet a splendid beginning had been made, though it was only a beginning. Are we going to stop short at this point ? Shall we not rather insist that our national distresses afford a reason for pushing on with the work, rather than for leaving it incomplete, like a building which is allowed to fall into decay because the builder cannot afford to roof it ?

An ancient adage tells us that it is lawful to learn even from an enemy. And it is instructive to remember how Prussia laid the foundations of her future greatness in the days of disaster. A poor State of the second rank, she had been conquered by

Napoleon (1806), stripped of half of her territory, and forced to pay a heavy indemnity. Yet when she set to work to reconstruct her national life, almost her first undertaking was the creation of a better educational system, and the establishment of two great universities. Upon this foundation, by drawing upon the trained brain-power of her people, she built her mastery in science, from which followed her industrial triumphs, as well as the military strength which she was to misuse so terribly. For the Britain of 1923, as for the Prussia of 1807, the undeveloped brain-power of the nation is the greatest available asset, which it will be fatal to neglect. To reduce our expenditure in this field would be as false economy as that of the farmer who should refuse to spend money in manuring his fields. We must make the profession of the teacher sufficiently attractive to enlist the services of men and women fit for their august task. We must make the ladder of ascent broad enough to accommodate every child of ability. We must provide training for adult citizens who desire it. We must ensure that the universities, which are the training grounds of the *élite*, are not so starved that they will be impotent to perform their high functions. All this must be done with an anxious economy, so that it shall burden the national exchequer as little as possible. And both for this reason, and in order that we may avoid a sterile uniformity, we must encourage "private enterprise" to come to the aid of the State in every practicable way. Now, more than ever before, is the opportunity for the pious founder; and, despite our national difficulties, there is enough wealth in private hands to do wonders in this field if a sufficient stimulus were given. We shall later suggest a possible way in which such a stimulus might be given.

What is true of education is equally true of public

health. Though we cannot proceed as rapidly as we might have done if there had been no war, the campaign against the slum has become more rather than less urgent; for physical unfitness is a greater cause of national impoverishment than even the burden of debt. It is needless to set forth a detailed programme of action in this field: enough that, while recognizing the need for the most watchful economy, Liberalism insists that a reduction of expenditure in this field would be sheer folly; and that a wise increase of expenditure may prove to be the most truly economical course. In this crisis of the nation's fortunes our highest duty to the future is to ensure that the rising generation is, so far as we can contrive, made physically and mentally fit for the heavy burdens it will have to bear.

V. THE FULFILMENT OF DEMOCRACY

We turn next to spheres of reform in which the problem of finance presents no such grave embarrassments as in education and public health: the spheres of political and industrial reorganization, wherein Liberalism recognizes that it will find its greatest future tasks.

Before we can hope for success in any large measures of social reform, we must ensure that our political machinery is adequate for its work. Already it is showing signs of breaking down, and is losing the public confidence that it once enjoyed. Parliament has too many things to do to be able to do any of them well. It cannot adequately control the Cabinet, which has become its master rather than its servant. The Cabinet in its turn is overburdened, with the consequence that permanent officials wield in a growing degree that unchecked authority which is described by the term "bureaucracy." The larger the functions which we impose upon our governing machine, the more clearly these tendencies must display themselves; and we must never forget this danger when we demand that "Government" or "the State" shall assume fresh powers in order to deal with this evil or that.

How is this dangerous state of things to be amended? How is our system to be made capable of dealing with the increased demands which will certainly be made upon it during the next generation? Unless we can answer these questions satisfactorily, we shall find that our engine will break down under the load which we require it to draw.

We cannot here attempt to discuss in detail the very large problems which these questions raise. It must suffice to catalogue very briefly the political reforms which most Liberals feel to be necessary.

1. The first need is to restore confidence in the efficiency of Parliament as an effective reflection of the mind of the nation. This confidence has been undermined in the first place by the fact that one of the two Houses of Parliament is wholly unrepresentative, and includes a very large number of men whose sole title to be there is in many cases the fact that they are rich. Confidence has been undermined in the second place by the fact that the method of election even to the representative House is such as to make it possible that a party with a definite minority of votes can obtain a large majority of seats; while something like 70 per cent of the electors are conscious that they have not voted for anybody who sits at Westminster. It is evident that a reform of both Houses of Parliament is necessary.

The Labour party advocates the total abolition of the Second Chamber. There are very few Liberals who take this view; because it seems plain that in the congested state of public business it is impossible for a single chamber to find time for the adequate discussion of all the necessary legislation and, in the conditions in which legislative work has to be done in the House of Commons, it is often so scamped and hurried that some revision or reconsideration is indispensable.

The Liberal view is that the Second Chamber should be definitely less powerful than the House of Commons. Its essential function should be that of revision; and it should not have the power to reject finally or permanently measures supported by a clear majority in the popular House. This was secured by the Parliament Act of 1911, and no scheme of Second Chamber reform (such as most Conservatives would advocate) which would restore to a reformed House its old powers of absolute veto can be accepted. But the Parliament Act is insufficient. Since it leaves the House of Lords unreformed, and with a permanent Conservative majority, it deprives the nation of any real revising chamber when Conservative governments are in power; while, when Liberal and Labour governments are in power, their proposals can be held up for three years, and they can be compelled to waste the time of Parliament by passing the same measures thrice through all their stages. It is therefore necessary that there should be a drastic reform of the House of Lords, including the total abolition of a hereditary right to legislate, and the creation of a new type of assembly which will not be permanently and predominantly of one political complexion, or represent only vested interests. To such a reform the Liberal party is definitely committed. But space does not permit of any discussion of the form which the revised Second Chamber ought to assume.

Even more important is the restoration of the representative character of the House of Commons—if possible, on such a basis as will enable every elector to feel that his vote has not been wasted, but has helped to return somebody to Westminster. The only mode yet devised whereby such a result can be obtained is the abolition of single-member constituencies (which have only been general in Britain since 1885), and their replacement by large constituencies with from three to ten members, wherein the electors would be entitled to cast only one vote, but to indicate the order of their later preferences should their vote not be needed for the candidate of their first choice. This is the system of Proportional Representation by the single transferable vote. Its result would be that the balance of opinion in the House of Commons would much more nearly represent the balance of opinion in the country than it now does, and that intermediate shades of opinion would be much more fully represented than they now are.

The criticism commonly made against this system is that it would be incompatible with the existence of a strong government commanding a clear majority in the House of Commons. This criticism implies that Cabinet dictatorship over the House of Commons is indispensable, and that no government can be stable or efficient unless it is able to force through the House any measure upon which it has set its mind. But this is a false reading of our system. It is precisely the exaggerated dictatorship of the Cabinet which we desire to be rid of. In the mid-nineteenth century, when majorities were always small, and when party discipline was anything but rigid, no Cabinet dared to disregard the feeling of the House; and debates influenced votes, as they now seldom do. In a House elected by Proportional Representation these conditions would be restored. It would be impossible for a ministry to force a measure through by a threat of resignation; and it is probable that ministries would be retained in power so long as their administrative record was good, but that they would not necessarily resign if their legislative proposals were very substantially amended. The results of such a change would be altogether good. Administrative work would be more closely watched and criticized; the part played by Parliament in legislation would be more real; and debates would genuinely influence decisions.

II. Not only must the constitution of both Houses of Parliament be amended so as to make them more genuinely representative of the national mind: the procedure of Parliament must be improved, and it must be relieved of a great deal of the work it now scurries through, in order that the rest may be more efficiently performed.

We cannot here discuss in detail the necessary changes of procedure. But one substantial reform ought to be noted. In order that Parliament may be kept in touch with the regular work of the great departments, check their growing expenditure efficiently, and limit the increase of bureaucratic power, there should be a series of parliamentary standing committees for each of the principal departments. These committees should be endowed with large powers of inquiry, but they should not be placed in such a position as to enable them to undermine or override the responsibility of the minister-in-charge for the larger questions of policy.

More important than reform of procedure is the relief of Parliament by some kind of devolution. This can be effected in two ways. On the one hand what may be described as regional assemblies may be set up; and in the cases of Wales and Scotland such assemblies might well be so organized as to give some reflection to the distinctive national aims and characters of these countries. It may be desirable that these bodies should be elected *ad hoc*. But since they would mainly be concerned with the regulation and supervision of existing local authorities, it would probably be best that they should be constituted by indirect election from the County Councils and Borough Councils of a given area. Bodies thus constituted could be empowered to exercise some of the legislative functions of Parliament, especially in the conferment of powers upon local authorities; they could co-ordinate and supervise the work of these authorities, and undertake certain kinds of public work which would best be done on a larger scale than that of the municipal borough or the county area; and they would form a very valuable means of criticizing the proceedings of the great Government departments which come into contact with local authorities. The functions thus described would involve no decrease of the ultimate sovereign authority of Parliament, but they would relieve Parliament of a great deal of work which it does not do well; and they might be expected to lead to a real increase of efficiency in the performance of many vital public services such as education, the relief of destitution, the provision of good roads and efficient transport and of water supply.

An even greater relief to Parliament would be afforded by the establishment of bodies so constituted as to be able to deal efficiently with problems of a special order. This may be described as "functional devolution"; the form already described being "regional devolution." The outstanding illustration of such a system would be provided by the establishment of a National Industrial Council; to which we shall return later.

These are the most outstanding of the political or structural reforms which are necessary if our system is to work smoothly and if large measures of social reorganization are to be carried with general assent. They do not exhaust the list. The Cabinet itself needs reorganization, and in particular it ought to be reduced in size. The distribution of administrative functions among the great departments, and their relations with one another, need reconsideration. Many reforms are necessary in the structure and functions of local government, and particularly in the methods by which their funds are raised. But enough has been said to show that the task of organizing the machinery of democracy is still far from complete, and that in this sphere Liberalism recognizes the existence of many problems which must be solved as a means to the attainment of social health.

In truth, we have as yet taken only the first steps towards the creation of an effective system of self-government, such as will enable and encourage every public-spirited citizen to play his part in the forwarding of the common weal, and will let him feel that his efforts are not wasted. To create such a system has always been one of the supreme aims of Liberalism. It is an aim worth pursuing for its own sake. But it is still more worth pursuing as a means to a happier social order and a wider diffusion of well-being. To this, as the supreme aim of political action, all else must be subordinate; and the projects of social reform, to which we shall next turn, must be the main inspiration of Liberalism during the next generation.

VI. SOCIAL UNREST

What are the causes of the social unrest which is

the dominating fact of our time, and which forbids the harmonious national co-operation that is needful if we are to overcome our difficulties ?

It is due, says the average Conservative, to a sort of world-wide fever or mania, and the best chance of a cure lies in a period of rest or tranquillity, firmly but tactfully enforced. This mania, he would add, is partly the outcome of the general upheaval caused by the war, but is also partly due to the influence of wicked or fanatical agitators. If the problems of the moment can be wisely handled as they arise, and if all agitating movements can be damped down or quietly blanketed, the patient will recover in time, and things will go on much as they did in the past.

This diagnosis seems wholly unsatisfactory both to the Liberal and to the Labour man. They hold that social unrest is due to the existence of real and serious evils in the social order, which have become more apparent to our generation because it is an educated generation. The war and the troubles which have followed it have intensified the unrest in many ways, but they did not cause it. It is the duty of the community to find the means of removing the injustices from which unrest springs ; and until it does so, we shall have no peace. The solution of these problems, already urgent before the war, has become tenfold more urgent since the war.

But when the rival political physicians pass from diagnosis to prescription, they differ very widely indeed. Nothing, says the Socialist physician, will be of any avail short of a very drastic surgical operation. The patient needs a new brain, a new heart and a new stomach, and our theorists have a great many pretty (though contradictory) plans for supplying these : we can settle the details later ; in the meanwhile, let us get on with the operation—let us cut out the heart and the brain—let us get rid of capitalism and private enterprise. Anything short of this will only be a palliative, and things will go steadily from bad to worse until the great operation is completed. We must cease to trust to private initiative and private thrift, which have hitherto been the motive forces of the economic organism; we must replace them by some sort of community-control over all the economic processes, to be exercised either through government officials, or through elected committees of workers. That is the Socialist's ultimate solution for every problem.

The Liberal physician rejects this prescription as vigorously as he rejects the Conservative prescription. He believes that social health demands not a restriction of private enterprise, but an immense expansion of it. He refuses to believe in the existence of any single panacea for social ills. He holds that we have already made great progress towards social justice during the last hundred years, and that, in the main, the direction which further advance ought to take is pretty clearly marked. He recognizes the existence of many grave evils, and the need of a concerted and systematic attempt to overcome them. But they cannot be remedied by formulæ, but only by hard thinking, piece by piece.

What are, or what should be, the aims of Liberal policy in this sphere? We cannot discuss them in any detail, but they may be usefully grouped under four heads: (1) measures designed to remedy the maldistribution of the nation's wealth; (2) measures designed to give to all citizens that degree of security of life which is necessary for any real freedom; (3) measures designed to ensure that all who share in the creation of the national wealth shall feel that they are reasonably consulted as to the conditions under which they have to work, and are treated as citizens with minds and wills, not as mere tools; (4) measures designed to ensure the wise employment of the national resources, and the efficient working of those pivotal industries upon which all the rest depend. These four groups of questions largely overlap, as we shall see. But we shall take them, very briefly, in the order in which they have been set down above.

VII. THE MALDISTRIBUTION OF WEALTH

The most natural and obvious cause of social unrest is the spectacle of vast wealth lavishly expended alongside of penury and degradation. No reasonable man dreams of bringing about an exact equality in the distribution of wealth, or grudges his riches to the man who has earned them by exceptional vigour, foresight, and enterprise. But the inequalities of to-day are gross and flagrant. They seem to have little relation to the services rendered. These extremes must be rectified ere society can attain full health. But they must be rectified in ways which will not discourage enterprise or restrain freedom. There are four ways in which Liberal policy can deal, and has already in some degree dealt, with this problem.

1. The first is by *preventing "anti-social" methods of accumulating wealth* through the exploitation of the community. Many large fortunes have been made by such methods, and it ought not to be beyond the power of the community to forbid them, or at any rate, to restrict them within narrow limits.

One of the ways in which wealth may be accumulated at the cost of the community is by the formation of Trusts, Combines, or other monopolistic or quasi-monopolistic organizations. The danger of exploitation by such bodies can be guarded against if they are required (as the railways now are) to publish detailed accounts of their costings, earnings, and outgoings; and on the basis of these accounts a public department should have the power of fixing the maximum prices to be charged for the commodities thus produced, just as the rates and fares of the railways are fixed to-day. Under such a system the economies which trust-organization can often secure would be obtained, but they would be shared by the public; and the shareholders of these concerns would be prevented from heaping up wealth by overcharging the consumer.

A second form of anti-social wealth is the "unearned increment" that the owner of land derives, without any activity on his own part, from the growth of towns or the construction of railways or roads on or near his land; often enough this "unearned increment" is swollen by the practice of withholding land from use until it has reached an exorbitant price. A well-designed system of land taxation, such as Liberalism is committed to introduce, forms the best means of dealing with this mode of accumulating wealth at the public cost.

Again, much wealth is illegitimately acquired by financial trickery of various sorts which does nothing but harm to industry. It is the business of a sound system of commercial law to make these devices impossible; and there is need for a careful revision of the Companies Acts for the purpose of making unsound or dishonest flotation of companies impossible.

II. The second mode of rectifying the maldistribution of wealth is that of ensuring *a fair sharing of the product of each industry* between the factors engaged in it. In this regard substantial advances have already been made, partly by collective bargaining, partly by State intervention through

Trade Boards, and in other ways. There are, of course, very definite limits to the practicable increase of wages in any industry. They cannot be raised to such a pitch that the commodities produced are too dear to find a market; and there must be a sufficient margin of profit to attract a constant stream of capital, lacking which no industry can thrive. But subject to these conditions, labour ought to receive the maximum regular wage that the industry, taken as a whole, can bear.

There have been moments (as in the period following the recent boom) when the regular wage rates of labour were definitely higher than industry could bear. But in general it cannot be said that labour receives the maximum practicable wage, except in the most highly organized industries; and even in these, wage rates are necessarily fixed, in the main, in relation to the paying capacity of the weaker and less efficient concerns. If, as we have urged, the remuneration of labour included, in addition to the standard wage, a variable element bearing some proportion to the prosperity of individual concerns, the result would be twofold: on the one hand, labour as a whole would receive a larger share of the total product; on the other hand, by attracting the better workers to the better-managed concerns, such a system would penalize inefficiency, and every increase in efficiency means an increase of the wealth produced and of the share of it which labour can legitimately claim—and can obtain if the machinery of wage-adjustment is well designed. But the leaders of organized labour have set their faces against any such system, and this for three reasons. First, they fear that such a system might impair the worker's loyalty to his trade union by strengthening his loyalty to the concern in which he is employed. As things are, this is true, and it can only be mended if the trade union has its share in determining the variable element in the remuneration of labour as well as the standard wage. Secondly, they desire to protect the weaker workers even if this also involves protecting the weaker concerns and diminishing the nation's productive power; and, so long as the existing sense of insecurity overhangs the whole body of workers, this is a justifiable attitude. Thirdly, they suspect the good faith of all profit-sharing schemes; and, so long as these are wholly dependent upon the mere goodwill of the employer, the suspicion is not without foundation.

The belief is widespread among the workers in all industries that the employers will not grant a penny of increase voluntarily. This belief is justified in all but exceptional cases; and so long as this is so, conflict will continue to be incessant between the partner factors which ought to be co-operative. The difficulty can only be met (1) by the creation of trustworthy machinery, which will be accepted by both sides, not only for the periodical readjustment of wage rates, but also for the fixing of the principles upon which any schemes of a profit-sharing nature should be administered; and (what is even more important) (2) by supplying full knowledge to both sides as to the condition and prospects of the industry.

In regard to the first point, Liberal legislation has already pointed the way to a great advance by the institution of the Trade Boards, which have raised the level of wages in many industries. The main features of the Trade Board system, and more especially its power of making the rates which it fixes legally enforcible, are capable of extension to other industries wherein wage rates are regulated by collective bargaining between employers and employed.

But the Trade Boards themselves need, for full

efficiency, more knowledge of the facts than they can now obtain. And this illustrates the vital importance of our second point—adequate knowledge. It must be provided by law that every firm engaged in productive industry must confidentially communicate to an approved official (preferably an official of the Joint Industrial Council of the trade, if this exists) a periodical statement showing the amount spent on materials and other costs of production, on wages, on salaries, on commissions, on interest on various kinds of capital, etc. ; so that on the basis of these statements a generalized statement for the industry as a whole may be prepared. The accessibility of trustworthy knowledge of this kind would do more to promote understanding and confidence than anything else ; and it would make it possible to decide, with a very close approximation to exactitude, just what wage rates the industry as a whole could afford to pay without losing its markets or driving away capital.

But standard wage rates, fixed in this way, will apply to industries as a whole. They will represent the amount that the weaker firms are just able to pay. Stronger and better managed concerns will make larger profits ; and these, though mainly, will not be wholly due to the skill of their directors. It is but just that labour should obtain a share of such additional prosperity—especially since the prospect of such a share will stimulate the workers to increase their product or avoid waste. But such additional remuneration ought to be received as by right and not by grace of the employer ; and, since the conditions vary infinitely from one industry to another and no uniform system could be applied by law, the basis upon which these extra payments should be made ought to be fixed for an industry as a whole. Hence the possibility of advance in this direction depends upon the development of a system of industrial self-government, on which we shall touch later.

The just determination of wage rates, which involves the just distribution of the product of industry, is perhaps the most important way of securing a healthy distribution of wealth. But it leaves almost untouched all that vast body of "unearned" wealth derived from investments, the existence of which, and the way in which it is often used, form perhaps the chief stimulating causes of unrest.

III.—In a very large degree *taxation can be utilized as a means of reducing the grosser inequalities of wealth*; and it has been thus used by Liberal policy on a large scale. As we have earlier seen, the graduated income-tax and super-tax, combined with the Death Duties, have in fact imposed upon the wealthier classes the bulk of the national burdens, and have made possible the rendering to the poorer classes of many services (such as education) for which they pay little or nothing directly. Death Duties, in particular, have done much to break up swollen fortunes. It is true that large fortunes are both bigger and more numerous than they were before the Death Duties were introduced; but they would have been yet bigger and yet more numerous but for the operation of the Death Duties. There is room for a still further increase of Death Duties, especially on the largest fortunes. But apart from this, it would seem that we have reached the limit within which taxation can advantageously be used as a means of redistributing wealth. The income-tax is higher than the economic interests of the nation would dictate. And in any case it is undesirable that the instrument of taxation should be deliberately employed for such a purpose. It is much better to aim at a just distribution than at an enforced redistribution.

IV.—There remains a method of dealing with swollen fortunes which was advocated fifty years ago by a great Liberal thinker, John Stuart Mill, but which has never been put into operation. This is the *limitation of the right of bequest*, so as to ensure that no one shall enjoy a vast inherited fortune, which he has done nothing to earn, but which gives him a dangerous power over his neighbours. In approaching this subject it is necessary to beware of the danger of undermining one of the most powerful motives to energy and thrift—the natural and laudable desire to provide for one's children, and to safeguard them against the accidents of life.

Two schemes have been put forward, both of which keep this necessity in view. The object of the first is to secure that the inheritors should only have a life-interest in their inheritance. It proposes that (after the State has taken its toll of Death Duties) the whole of the testator's estate should be treated as a trust, the income of which only would be enjoyed by those to whom it was bequeathed. On the death of the first generation the State would take a second and heavier toll, but the trust would continue. On the death of the second generation the whole residuum would pass to the State. In this way, the whole of the existing capital of the country would pass into the hands of the State in two generations, though new capital, created later, would remain in private hands. The scheme is essentially a Socialist scheme. Its supreme disadvantage is the disadvantage of all Socialist proposals—that they sacrifice the greatest benefit which comes from the private ownership of capital, namely the fact that such capital can be and is risked and lost in all sorts of venturesome experiments whereby progress is achieved. All the vast body of capital which would under this scheme be locked up in trusts could not be risked in this way; and the loss to the community would be incalculable.

Far simpler, and far more rational, is the second scheme, which had the support of President Roosevelt. It proposes that testators should simply be prohibited by law from bequeathing more than a defined sum to any private person; but, subject to this single restriction, it would leave the rich man free to distribute the whole of his estate as he thought fit, and it would impose no limitation upon the amount which he might bequeath to public objects. The maximum sum to be bequeathed was fixed by Roosevelt at $100,000, or £20,000. This is enough to provide the legatee with a very comfortable income; enough to enable him to devote himself to public service or to follow any of those useful careers which almost necessitate private means, such as the disinterested pursuit of learning, or the life of exploration; enough to give him a good start in business. The subject has been very little discussed; and before a definite figure could be fixed, its effects upon industrial organisation would have to be carefully considered. But the virtues of such a method are great. It would create a leisured class of moderate means, apt for many kinds of public service. It would encourage the endowment of public institutions, universities, schools, and hospitals, from private resources which would give them character and independence. It would effectively break up big accumulations of wealth, without depriving their creators of the right to enjoy them during life and to make reasonable provision for their children. It would stimulate rather than repress individual enterprise. The whole subject has still to be explored; but it is probable that along these lines lies the true solution of the problem of dealing with the grosser inequalities in the distribution of wealth.

VIII. SECURITY OF LIVELIHOOD

It has been the constant refrain of this little book that a reasonable security is an essential condition of freedom and peace. That is so in international relations. It is equally so in the industrial sphere. There is no cause of social unrest more potent than the haunting sense of insecurity which overhangs the mass of working people from childhood to the grave.

Liberalism entered upon a systematic attempt to remedy this evil during the years immediately preceding the war, when it established Old Age Pensions, National Health Insurance, and Unemployment Insurance. This work had barely begun when it was interrupted by the war. To continue and perfect it must be one of our earliest tasks.

The greatest source of insecurity is unemployment. But since, over a series of years, the average number of unemployed is only 4 per cent of the working population, the problem is a manageable one. On the exceptional problem created by the distresses of 1921 and 1922 we have already said something: it is a problem of such dimensions that it would have broken down any system suitable for normal times, and the national system had been so recently brought into full operation that, having no reserves behind it, it inevitably collapsed. But here it is our business to consider how Liberalism ought to deal with the normal problem, when we return to something like normal conditions.

Prevention is better than cure; and if we could get rid of unemployment altogether, or greatly reduce its volume, by evening out the recurrent booms and slumps of what is called the "trade cycle," this would plainly be the best solution. Something can undoubtedly be done in this direction if the organizers of industry give thought to the matter, if government and municipal purchases are wisely distributed, and if credit and currency can be handled with a foresight almost impossible in our present state of knowledge. But it is too much to hope for a complete cure, in a country which depends, as Britain does, upon its foreign trade, which may at any moment be disturbed by unpredictable and uncontrollable factors. We must contemplate the necessity of providing always for an average 3 or 4 per cent. of the working population, distributed over all the industries, but especially numerous in those of them which suffer from seasonal fluctuations.

There will be no satisfactory solution of the problem until the unemployed man is assured of a scale of maintenance proportionate to his normal standard of living, so that he may be saved from the necessity of breaking up his home. A fair scale for this purpose would be 50 per cent of the unemployed man's normal wages in the case of a bachelor, together with additional allowances for a married man's wife and family, the whole not to amount to more than 75 per cent of the normal wage. How is this to be secured?

It is not secured under our existing system of State insurance, even as it would work in normal times; for a State system must necessarily be based upon a flat rate of contributions and a flat rate of benefit, which must necessarily be computed upon the basis of the wages received by the lowest grades of labour. This limitation is almost inherent in any State system. Partly for this reason, it has been proposed that State insurance should be abandoned, and that in its place there should be a system of insurance by industries, each industry supporting its own unemployed. This project has received the weighty support of the Geddes Committee, which thought it saw its way to a great economy in the abolition of the Labour Exchanges which have to be maintained as part of the machinery of State insurance. But in fact a system based entirely upon insurance by industries is out of the question. It is impossible to draw hard-and-fast lines between the industries. Take, for example, the case of a labourer who works part of the year for a builder, and part of the year for an engineering contractor. Which industry is to pay for his maintenance when he is out of work? Moreover, a system based upon industries would be very unfair to those industries (such as building) which are in the nature of things subject to great fluctuations of employment. Under a State system the trades which suffer least help the trades which suffer most. A system of State insurance giving a minimum uniform rate of unemployment benefit is the necessary foundation upon which more adequate provision can be raised.

Already in one great firm and in one substantial industry the problem has been largely solved by taking the State system as the basis, and adding to its benefits up to the scale (50–75 per cent of the normal wage) already indicated. And this is, beyond doubt, the mode in which a solution will be found: the State system, with its flat rate of contribution and of benefit, will provide the foundation; the organized industries will supplement the benefit up to a proper relation with every man's normal wage. In many industries, where the burden of unemployment is normally light, the cost of this supplementary provision would be exceedingly small: an addition of something like 1 per cent on the wages bill would probably cover it. The burden would be heavier in other industries, but it would be prohibitive in none. And the security which it would bring, and the removal of a sense of injustice which would result from it, would immensely outweigh the cost. This system of supplementary provision could not, indeed, be made to cover the whole ground: there would be many men hovering on the margin of two industries whom it might at first be impossible to bring under such a system. But even they would at least have the State benefits to fall back upon. And in any case, a reasonable security would have been attained for the great bulk of the industrial workers of the country.

In the same way, and by the same methods, provision should also be made against old age—again in supplement to the pensions provided by the State: at no large cost supplementary maintenance allowances could be provided, as by right, to men who after long service had reached the age of 60, and were no longer capable of full work. And the knowledge that old age was provided for would afford the greatest stimulus to thrift, especially if (what is, in any case, necessary) the shortsighted provisions of the State pension system which penalize the man who has saved were abrogated.

By these means a reasonable security can be given to the men and women who spend their lives in the industrial service of the community; and the worst evil of the existing economic order can be overcome. When this difficulty has been healed, one of the chief obstacles to wholehearted work will have been removed, and a new motive for thrift will have been provided.

But there is one condition which is necessary for the successful working of such a system. The industries must be organized. They must have controlling councils, upon which employers and employed are equally represented, to administer these schemes, as well as to discuss wage rates and the conditions of labour. And these councils or boards must have the power to enforce the system upon which they have agreed, throughout the industry, and to levy contributions from all concerns in the industry, in proportion to the number of men of different grades whom they employ. Not only this, but they must have before them full knowledge of the broad facts about the industry, such as would be provided by the periodical returns already described. In other words, a system of industrial self-government, and a reasonable publicity of accounts (generalized for industries as a whole), are essential for a solution of the problem of security, as they are also for a solution of the problem of distribution.

IX. INDUSTRIAL SELF-GOVERNMENT

It appears, then, that the creation of a system of industrial self-government which will relieve Parliament and the Cabinet of the immediate (though not of the ultimate) responsibility for the definition of industrial policy lies at the root of any real progress towards a Liberal solution of our problems. And this conclusion is in accord with the genius of Liberalism, which always desires to entrust the functions of regulation to those who are most immediately concerned, rather than to attempt to deal with them by the direct intervention of politicians and administrative officials. More than eighty years ago, when the French and the English in Canada were at one another's throats, and their conflicts were ruining the prosperity of their common country, the genius of Liberalism, speaking through Lord Durham, thrust upon them the responsibility for managing their own affairs in equal partnership. "It is your own welfare, the welfare of both of you, that is at stake," Lord Durham in effect proclaimed; "and while you are striving for supremacy the sources of your well-being are being stopped. Forget your quarrels: your fate is in your own hands; we give you the means of self-government; it is now your own fault if you do not find a *modus vivendi*." The result was that Canada won harmony, and sprang in a generation from an all but derelict colony into a great and free State, more eagerly loyal to the greater Commonwealth of which she is a member than ever she had been before.

That is the spirit of Liberalism; and the old recipe of freedom and responsibility is as apt for the solution of friction between Labour and Capital as for that happily forgotten friction between French and English colonists, who soon learnt to pursue their common welfare in comradeship instead of seeking a ruinous mastery of one over the other. But the proper field of self-government—of decisions by votes and discussions—is the same in industry as in other spheres: it ought to be concerned with the problems of justice in human relationship, not with technical questions involving special knowledge or peculiar gifts.

We have elsewhere shown how Liberalism would desire to see the practice of self-government developed (within its appropriate limits) at three distinct levels in the industrial world: in the individual factory or mine, for the avoidance of hardships and the adjustment of discipline without friction; in particular industries as a whole, for the definition of wage rates, the hours and conditions of labour, the methods of profit-sharing or payment by results, and the treatment of the problems of security; and, finally, in the field of industrial policy as a whole, for the co-ordination of the policies pursued by particular industries, and for the relief and guidance of Parliament and the Government.

At what point can we best start in striving to develop such a system by political action? Clearly not in the factory, where conditions vary so widely that no generalized provisions would be practicable. In particular industries we can do much, by encouraging and strengthening Trade Boards where they exist, and by giving them a statutory right to collect and use the information which we have seen to be necessary; and also, in some of the more highly organized industries, by strengthening the Joint Industrial Councils where they are working well—giving them the right to obtain compulsory powers for dealing with wage questions or the problem of unemployment when they are able to reach agreement. We cannot, by legislative action, force into existence a cut-and-dried scheme if the industries are not ready to work it, or if they find a difficulty in defining their range. At this stage, legislation must for these purposes be of a permissive character.

But there is one thing which we can do immediately. We can constitute by statute a National Industrial Council, representative of employers and employed in all industries, and entrust to it the challenging task of working out a solution of our problems, of stimulating particular industries to organize themselves, and of laying down the general lines of policy upon the various aspects of the industrial problem. That is a first step wholly in accord with the traditions of Liberalism: it ought to be (as indeed it is) the first plank in the Liberal industrial platform.

X. THE MANAGEMENT OF NATIONAL ASSETS AND OF BASIC INDUSTRIES

It has been the constant burden of this book that the community not only may, but must, intervene in the industrial process for the purpose of ensuring that justice is secured in human relationships, though not for controlling the technical sides of industry. But there are some sections or aspects of the industrial life of the nation in which intervention may possibly have to be carried further than this. Where the use of essential and irreplaceable national assets is involved, the community may have to take measures to ensure that these assets are not wastefully used, or that the power over them which private owners possess is not employed in such a way as to restrict harmfully the action of other citizens. And in the case of those industries (especially the industries concerned with transport or the supply of power) which are fundamental to the conduct of all other industries, it may be necessary for the community to ensure that they are conducted in such a way as not to be liable to interruption, and as not to prey upon what may (from this point of view) be described as the secondary industries.

First among the essential and irreplaceable assets of the nation comes the land, upon the use of which all activities whatsoever depend. Private ownership of land has many advantages, and in any case it is so deeply rooted that it cannot readily be overthrown. But it must not be used in such a way as to hold to ransom the productive activities of the nation. We have long since got rid of the idea that "a man may do what he likes with his own." A man may do with his own—with his own bodily strength, or with his own possessions—only those things that do not interfere with the well-being of his neighbour; this is true of all things, but it is especially true of land, the ownership of which gives to the man who possesses it more power over his neighbours than any other kind of possession.

To the same category belong the waters on the surface of the land: control over these must not be used as a means of holding the community to ransom, nor must private ownership be allowed to forbid their being used in the most advantageous way for the provision of power to the community. Again, the mineral resources which lie beneath the land are not only irreplaceable assets essential to national prosperity, they are wasting assets, which will be exhausted within a measurable period; and the community ought to ensure that they are utilized as wisely and economically as may be.

Finally, the basic industries which are concerned with the provision of transport and of power are so vital to the successful working of the whole industrial organism that the reasons for intervening to ensure their successful working are infinitely stronger than the reasons for intervening in other industries. In the case of transport this has long been recognized. The community has taken into its own hands the control of posts, telegraphs, and telephones; it has taken over the management of the roads, and maintains them at the public expense; nearly all docks are under public management; and the railways, ever since the days of their beginnings, have been subject to a far closer control than any other industries whatsoever—not only because they are monopolies, but chiefly because they are a vital part of the nation's equipment. The necessity for a closer supervision of the conditions under which power is provided has been more slowly realized than the necessity of regulating transport, because it is only in the last two generations that artificially generated power has become essential for the conduct of almost all industries.

It is therefore necessary that we should examine what ought to be the policy of Liberalism in regard to the use and control of irreplaceable national assets, and in regard to the conduct of the basic industries upon which all productive activity depends. And at the outset the broad principle may be laid down that, so far as possible, the interventions of the State should be limited to supervision and regulation, and that (subject to this regulation) the inventive and creative power of individual initiative should be given free play.

In the case of land, there are two main problems to be solved. The first arises from the fact that, as the amount of land available is very definitely limited, many of its owners are tempted to use their control over it for the purpose of enriching themselves at the expense of the community by withholding it from use, or refusing to sell it, until they can obtain an exorbitant price. And this tendency stands in the way of many needful advances—the removal of slums, the creation of small holdings, the replanning of towns. As things are, it often seems to be the interest of the owner *not* to allow his land to be used in the way which would be most advantageous to the community, until he is paid an exorbitant ransom. The second problem arises from the fact that, partly for the reasons already given, partly because of the survival of feudal notions and practices, and partly because the transfer of land is extraordinarily cumbrous and costly, it is often extremely difficult for men of enterprise and initiative to gain access to the land which they need for the development of their enterprise. This means that the existing land system does not encourage private enterprise, but rather inhibits and restrains it.

The method of dealing with this problem which is advocated by Socialists is the acquisition of all land by the State. And many Liberals feel that the case for nationalization is, in theory, stronger in regard to land than in regard to anything else, just because the use of land is essential for all activities, private and public. But there are three very powerful arguments against this solution which seem to be fatal to its adoption within any period which we can foresee. The first is the obvious fact that the process of acquiring all the land of the country would be so complicated and difficult that it is not to be thought of if any other way of overcoming the admitted difficulties of the present system can be devised. The second is that no one can contemplate without alarm the consequences of placing the administration of all land, urban and rural, in the hands of a government department. And the third is the testimony of all experience, that the pride of land ownership forms an extraordinarily powerful motive to effort and thrift. In theory, the holder of land ought to be satisfied with security of tenure. In practice he is never content with this: witness the eagerness of the State tenants of New Zealand to turn their perfectly secure holdings into freeholds. In all countries there is no body of men who work harder, show greater thrift, or are more independent and self-respecting than those who own a little land.

Land nationalization, whatever its attractions in theory, would in truth only get rid of the existing difficulties at the price of substituting another set of difficulties which would probably be still more harmful. And the ends desired can be secured far more satisfactorily by other means, which form an essential element in Liberal policy. In the first place, the purchase and sale of land must be made (so far as possible) as easy and cheap as the purchase and sale of other forms of property; and all restrictions, such as are involved in entails, must be abrogated. This is the policy of "free trade in land." In the second place, existing modes of land tenure must be greatly simplified, and the injustices which attend some forms of leasehold must be got rid of; something has already been done in this respect by the recent monumental Land Act for which Lord Birkenhead was finally responsible. In the third place, all public authorities must be given large powers of compulsory purchase at reasonable prices, based upon the actual value of the land to the seller: thus county councils must be enabled to purchase at an economic price all the land needed to meet the demand for small holdings, or for housing schemes; town councils must be enabled to buy up the sites of slums, or the areas needed for civic improvements, or for large housing schemes even beyond their own borders, at such prices as will not impose a permanent burden upon the ratepayer. And since it is often difficult for these authorities to raise in the money market sufficient funds to pay for their purchases in cash without paying excessive interest, there is much to be said for empowering them to pay in bonds to be issued by the Treasury, the interest, with a sinking fund, being guaranteed by the authority concerned. In this way national credit would be made available for public improvements; the capital funds available for industrial development would not be drawn upon; and the seller of land, though he would not get cash, would get a security which would be far more readily marketable in case of need than the land itself. The fourth reform which is needed would be even more efficacious than the foregoing: the existing system of rating and taxing land must be revised in such a way as to penalize, instead of rewarding, the man who fails to put his land to profitable use. As things are, the man who erects a valuable building on his land at once has his rates greatly increased; while the man who leaves his land idle pays no rates at all. He is therefore tempted to withhold his land from use until he can get a necessity-price; but when he has thus mulcted the community, he pays nothing in return; it is the new purchaser who has to face high rates, as soon as he begins to make a good use of the derelict land for which he has paid a fancy price. The problem of dealing with this situation is not an easy one. But it lies at the root of the land question; and Liberalism is pledged to deal with it. The policy we have described is, of course, incompatible with a policy of land nationalization. But the Labour party proclaims its adherence to both of these contradictory alternatives.

The coal-mining industry presents an interesting example of the combination of the two factors necessitating State intervention which we have been discussing. On the one hand it is concerned with the exploitation of an essential national asset—an asset, moreover, which (unlike the land) is destroyed by use, and therefore ought to be utilized with a wise economy. On the other hand the industry is one of the foundations of national prosperity, being essential to the conduct of other industries. On both grounds there is strong justification for State intervention if the industry is not working satisfactorily, or if the coal supplies are being wastefully exploited. During the last twenty years it has become obvious that both of these conditions have been fulfilled. The industry is working so unsatisfactorily that we have had repeated strikes, involving a grave interruption of most other industries; while we are informed, on the high authority of Sir Richard Redmayne, that the existing organization of the industry cannot be defended.

Since the last strike, a vary interesting experimend has been made in the division of the total product on an agreed basis between capital and labour and we may hope that this may lead to a better relation between the two co-operdting factors, especially as it involves (what no other industry has yet secured) a periodical publication or all the essential facts about the condition of the industry. But even if this result follows, nothing has yet been done to avoid the loss or waste of coal by a bad distribution of pits, and by difficulties about way-leaves; and very little has been done to protect the workers against unemployment in times of bad trade, or to ensure that they are effectively consulted, through their representatives, in regard to the conditions under which they have to work. And this makes it necessary that the community should consider and deal with the organization of the industry if it intends to avoid future trouble leading to the dislocation of the whole industrial system.

The cure suggested by the Labour party is their universal panacea—the nationalization of the industry as a whole, so that every mine manager should become a government official, and every miner a public servant. But the conditions under which the industry is carried on vary so widely that any uniform and centralized system would seem to be unworkable. And the possibility of working many mines upon an economic basis depends so largely upon skill in organization and marketing and upon watchful economy that it would seem to be dangerous to weaken the motives to good management. The profit-making motive may be a sordid one, as Labour idealists assure us. But it works; while the motive of public service (by which, we are told, it ought to be replaced) is not always incompatible, even among men in whom it is quite genuine, with a certain slipshodness in the handling of funds for which they are not personally liable. There are many mines so near the margin of solvency that a very slight reduction in the watchfulness of their managers would make them unworkable, and the coal they contain would be wasted. On these grounds it seems desirable to retain private enterprise in the actual management of mines.

But there is one function in the business of coal-getting wherein the enterprise and watchfulness of private ownership do not seem to produce, or to be capable of producing, any very profitable results. This is the function of the royalty owner, whose duties are confined to the granting of leases to mining companies, and the collection of royalties of so much a ton on the coal they extract. In this case the arguments in favour of the acquisition of these properties by the State seem to be overwhelming. They are, in fact, so convincing that the late Coalition government accepted the proposal, though it did nothing to carry it into effect.

If all the coal under ground, known and unknown, were acquired by the State, and paid for by the issue of bonds bearing a fixed rate of interest, it would become possible to use the power of granting leases as a means of bringing about a real reorganization of the industry, without any interference with private enterprise: the State would have in its hands a powerful weapon wherewith to compel the mining companies to group themselves in an economically sound way, and to provide such conditions of work as are necessary for the protection of the workers; while, by graduating its scale of royalties according to the richness and accessibility of the coal seams, it could to some extent equalize the conditions between different coalfields. The administration of this vast public estate should not, however, be placed in the hands of a government department under a politician chosen because of his opinions about the House of Lords or Tariff Reform, and subject only to the criticism of an overpressed Parliament. It should be entrusted to an expert Commission set up by Act of Parliament, and enjoying a good deal of freedom under the terms of the Act. By this means the community would be enabled, without sacrificing the driving force of private enterprise, to ensure that an essential national asset was not wastefully used, and that the work of exploiting it was carried on under such conditions as would satisfy all the reasonable demands of those engaged in it.

As we have already noted, a system of this kind would be equally applicable (with suitable modifications) for the management of our inadequate supply of water power, which, just because of its inadequacy, we ought to utilize far more fully than we now do.

The railways present an example—indeed, the supreme example—of an industry which is of vital importance for the prosperity of all other industries. For that reason they have been brought under a system of very strict State control; and there is no industry in which stronger arguments can be put forward in favour of national ownership. Liberalism has never, in principle, been opposed to the nationalization of the railways: Mr. Gladstone was actually the first advocate of railway nationalization, as long ago as 1844. But two reasons have stood in the way of the adoption of this measure. One was the belief that the competition of rival lines for the custom of the travelling public made for cheapness and efficiency. This argument has been destroyed by the recent amalgamation of all the railways of the country into four great systems. It is maintained, apparently with justice, that these amalgamations, while largely destroying competition, will bring about great economies and increased efficiency. If this is so, it may safely be asserted that they represent merely a stage on the way to a national system. The second ground of objection to national ownership is the fear that administration by a government department would lead to formalism, red tape, and inefficiency, and would bring the danger of mischievous political interferences. The experience of some other countries shows that there is real ground for these fears. But they would be largely nullified if, instead of being placed under a government department, a unified railway system were put under the direction of a powerful Commission whose constitution and functions would be defined by an Act of Parliament, and might be revised when necessary by a revision of the Act; and which would exercise, under the Act, a large degree of independent authority. This would free Parliament from direct responsibility for the control of the normal working of the system—a responsibility which it is incapable of meeting; but it would leave to Parliament the ultimate responsibility, since the Commission would exist by its legislative act. At the same time Government would not be a direct party in any dispute which might arise between the Commission and its employees; and it would be able—as in all industrial difficulties it ought to be able—in the last resort to intervene as an impartial arbiter.

On such a plan a national railway system might be organized which would be free from most of the defects of direct government control. It is probable that such a system will eventually come into existence. But the time for its establishment has not yet arrived. The new system of the four great groups, just set on foot, must be given a full and fair opportunity of testing itself; and the problem of railway administration is, for that reason, not a problem of immediate urgency.

We have briefly discussed the three questions of the land, the mines, and the railways because they are the outstanding cases in which a degree of State intervention more far-reaching than is necessary in most other industries will, for various reasons, have to be undertaken. They do not exhaust the category: afforestation and the supply of electric power may be named as other instances in which a substantial enlargement of the functions of the State may be necessary. But the three outstanding cases which we have discussed sufficiently serve to illustrate the spirit in which Liberalism ought to approach problems of this order. It ought to be ready to recognize the need for an increased degree of community-control in regard to industries or interests which are vital to the prosperity of the nation. It ought to avoid any rigid uniformity of method in dealing with these problems, such as all the rival Socialist schemes imply, but should seek to work out in each case the form of control appropriate to the circumstances. It ought, in establishing such schemes of control, to strive to retain to the maximum the creative and inventive power of private enterprise. And it ought to avoid the loading of Government and Parliament with new and inappropriate functions which they are incapable of performing efficiently.

In recognizing the need for large changes in these spheres, and especially in regard to the land, Liberalism will find itself in sharp conflict with Conservatism. In repudiating any rigid uniformity of method, in striving to retain the driving force of private enterprise, and in resisting direct control by the ordinary machinery of government, Liberalism will find itself in equally sharp conflict with Socialism. In this sphere, as in all others, the clear opposition of each of the three angles of our political triangle to the other two is very obvious.

XI. CONCLUSION

The survey of the immediate tasks of reform and of the way in which Liberalism approaches them, which has been attempted in these pages, is by no means complete. Many questions of high importance have been left untouched; no single question has been thoroughly explored. It is indeed impossible, in a little book like this, to cover the whole of the ground. This may seem easy to those who are content with sweeping formulæ and vague sentimentalisms. But the whole fascination of politics, seriously regarded, is that the problems which it presents are infinitely complex, demand hard thinking and sound knowledge, and cannot be solved by fluent phrases.

Our purpose in these pages has not been to set forth a cut-and-dried Liberal programme. The writer has no authority for such a task; and, in any case, detailed and cut-and-dried programmes are always dangerous and misleading, because they disregard the continually fluctuating circumstances with which practical politics have to deal. There is, indeed, scarcely any measure advocated in these pages which has not been accepted as a part of Liberal policy in the pronouncements of recognized leaders or the decisions of representative party gatherings. But our purpose has not been merely to catalogue these proposals, or even to present them as a coherent whole by showing their relation to one another. Our purpose has rather been to use them as the means of defining and illustrating the spirit in which Liberalism approaches the inspiring and bewildering problems of our day; to show that its attitude is not merely negative and critical, but that it is inspired by a positive and constructive ideal, as sharply opposed to that of Conservatism on the one hand as to that of Socialism on the other hand; and to demonstrate that in the triangle of modern parties the angle of Liberalism is as definite and as hopeful as that of its rivals.

The ultimate inspiration of this ideal is the same as it has always been, a belief in Liberty as the surest means of securing human progress; and for that reason the aims of the Liberal of to-day are not in conflict with the aims of the Liberal of 1830 or of 1880, but are the natural outcome and sequel of earlier aspirations and achievements. We believe that Liberty in any real sense has not yet been fully secured either for nations or for individuals. We believe that it must rest upon a foundation of reasonable security which it is the duty of the community to organize. We believe that it is the business of the State, and the end of politics, to create and to maintain "the conditions without which a free exercise of the human faculties is impossible." These conditions have, assuredly, not yet been attained. As civilization becomes more complex, and as education enables men to give voice to their discontents and their aspirations, our conception of what is implied in these conditions must grow deeper and broader, and the magnitude of the task that lies before us must become more apparent. Since this is so, we must recognize that it is impossible to define an ultimate ideal. The forms in which we embody our ideal must change as the modes of civilization alter, and as our understanding of the problem deepens. Nevertheless the inspiration of the essential Liberal ideal of freedom, as something that can only be made real by co-operation in goodwill, remains the surest guide through the shifting labyrinth of national and international difficulties. The task of Liberalism is not ended; it is but just beginning; and if only it is wisely guided and courageously expounded, with it lies the hope of the future. To-day, more than ever, it is the true path of progress.

It is difficult to suggest a short list of books on the vast range of contemporary problems. "Essays in Liberalism" (Collins) cover the greater part of the ground, and should be read: the writers in this remarkable little book are experts on their subjects. On special topics, Gilbert Murray's "Foreign Policy" is a convenient, readable and cheap handbook. Keynes's "Economic Consequences of the Peace" and "A Revision of the Treaty" are important. Major Astor and others have issued a very valuable study on "The Third Winter of Unemployment. Mr. Seebohm Rowntree's "Industrial Unrest" and "The Way to Industrial Peace" should be read. Sir Lynden Macassey has collected much useful material in "Labour Policy, true and false." More general treatments are given in Masterman's "New Liberalism," Muir's "Liberalism and Industry" and Elliott Dodd's "Liberalism in Action."

INDEX